THE ELUSIVE QUEST

The Struggle for Equality
of
Educational Opportunity

THE ELUSIVE QUEST

The Struggle for Equality
of
Educational Opportunity

Edwin Margolis
Judge of the New York State Court of Claims

Stanley Moses
Professor of Urban Planning Hunter College—CUNY

Foreword by Mario M. Cuomo
Governor of the State of New York

The Apex Press
New York

Copyright © 1992 by The Apex Press

Published by The Apex Press, an imprint of the Council on International and Public Affairs, 777 United Nations Plaza, New York, NY 10017 (212/953-6920)

Library of Congress Cataloging-in-Publication Data

Margolis, Edwin.
   The elusive quest : the struggle for equality of educational opportunity / Edwin Margolis and Stanley Moses.
      p.   cm.
   Includes bibliographical references (p.   ) and index.
   ISBN 0-945257-46-5
   1. Educational equalization—United States. 2. Educational equalization—New York (State)—Case studies. 3. Public schools—New York (State)—Finance—Case studies. 4. Politics and education—New York (State)—Case studies. I. Moses, Stanley. II. Title.
LC213.2.M37 1992   87-27076
370.19—dc19   CIP

Cover design by Warren Hurley
Typeset and printed in the United States of America

To
Mary Anne,
Lita, Daniel, and Josh

CONTENTS

TABLES

CHARTS

FOREWORD

One of the most important tasks of government is to ensure that every child, regardless of economic background, is given the same opportunity to succeed. The first step in this process is providing a quality education for all of our children, and this can only be achieved through equality in financing for our public schools.

The goal of fairness in educational financing is not easily obtained, however, and that "elusive quest" is accurately and eloquently described in this book. Judge Margolis and Professor Moses are particularly well qualified to tackle this difficult subject, and their experience allows them to provide an excellent description of the history of this quest, as well as unique insights into the inner workings of the legislative process.

The struggle for equality of educational opportunity is one which must be continued, and this book will be a valuable source of information and ideas for all who join our efforts to achieve fairness in our school financing system.

Albany, New York
March 1992

Mario M. Cuomo
Governor of the State of New York

PREFACE

I regard the publishing of this book as a very important contribution to the debate on educational policy in this nation, a subject with which I have been in close contact during my service with and chairmanship of the House Education and Labor Committee.

The authors have in a thorough and incisive manner demonstrated the obstacles to achieving equality of educational opportunity for the school children of this nation. They show how a combination of factors work to undermine efforts to lessen disparities between the financial resources made available for the education of poor children and those who come from more privileged circumstances.

Certainly it is a central value and belief of our American democracy that all children, regardless of race, religion, sex or family background, are entitled to the provision of the same public financial support for their schooling. Indeed, we consider it to be a central responsibility of government to administer and implement policies toward this end.

The history of educational policy in this country reflects the variety of arrangements created among local, state and federal governments to work toward implementing this goal. Sadly, the history of outcomes reflects the failure of governments—at all levels—to deliver on the promise of American democracy. Great differences in educational expenditures per pupil still exist througout the nation among school districts, within states and even between children in adjoining school district jurisdictions.

I was especially struck by their analysis of the variety and complexity of factors which combine to dictate that even the minimal goals of equality of fiscal opportunity cannot be obtained for poor children.

The U.S. Supreme Court, as well as the courts in most states, have rejected any constitutional or legal basis for equalization. At the same time, legislative and political systems at state and local levels, despite strong verbal support given to principles of equality, have retreated before the dictates of political bargaining and legislative compromise. And now, even the federal government, which at one time was a pacesetter regarding issues of compensatory education and equal opportunity, has abandoned this issue.

Although these may not be the best of times for equality advocates, I feel confident that the American public will not long tolerate the continuance of this disgraceful situation. The current situation violates our basic American good sense notion of justice and fair play. Especially poignant is the effect this has on children, who through no fault of their own, and for reasons related solely to the family backgrounds that they are born into, are deprived of some of the basic ingredients of fair treatment and equal opportunity.

This situation is an insult to our democratic heritage and our ideals about America. I am sure that as public consciousness becomes raised, we will at all levels of government, local, state and federal, once more pay greater attention to this blemish on our democracy.

I wish to express my appreciation and admiration of the authors for their painstaking and effective analysis of a complex situation. They describe the dilemmas of the situation in a reasoned and systematic manner. They do not make light of the restraints stemming from political reality, governmental administration and judicial interpretation. While their tone is objective, they are never deaf to the moral and human implications of their subject. In so doing, they have made an important contribution by pointing us toward the direction we must go if we are ever to succeed in achieving equal educational opportunity for all American school children.

Augustus F. Hawkins,
Former Chairman,
House Education
and Labor Committee,
U.S. Congress

ACKNOWLEDGMENTS

This book could not have been developed without the generous help and assistance of many people. Our direct access to many practitioners, advisors and decision makers in the fascinating field of educational finance, and their gracious and candid acceptance of us, opened areas of investigation that are generally hidden from researchers.

The problem with acknowledgments is that some very important and helpful people are invariably omitted. To those people we apologize for the oversight. However, we do wish to express our appreciation to the following individuals who spent considerable time imparting their wisdom and experience to us. (Positions stated are those held at the time of interview.)

Steve Allinger, Legislative Coordinator for Education Committee, New York State Assembly

Arvid Burke, formerly Director of Research at New York State Teachers Association and Professor of Education, State University of New York at Albany

Edward Cupoli, Chief Economist, Ways and Means Committee, New York State Assembly

Henrik N. Dullea, Director of State Operations, Office of the Governor, State of New York

Arthur O. Eve, Deputy Speaker of the New York State Assembly

Stanley Fink, Speaker of the New York State Assembly

Cornelius J. Foley, Assistant Secretary for Education and Local Government, Office of the Governor, State of New York

Gerald Freeborne, Deputy Commissioner for Elementary, Secondary, and Continuing Education, New York State Education Department

Jacob D. Fuchsberg, formerly Judge of the New York State Court of Appeals

Bertram Gross, Distinguished Professor Emeritus, Hunter College, City University of New York

Thomas F. Green, Professor of Philosophy and Education, Syracuse University

Ruth Henihan, Coordinator of Education and Special Information and System Services, New York State Education Department

Robert S. Herman, former New York State Deputy Budget Director and Professor of Administration, State University of New York at Albany

Thomas Y. Hobart, President, New York State United Teachers (AFL-CIO)

Amy Herz Juvilier, Judge of the Criminal Court of the City of New York

Daniel Kinley, Director of Legislative Services, New York State School Boards Association

Arthur J. Kremer, Chairman, Ways and Means Committee, New York State Assembly

Norman R. McConney, Sr., Chief of Staff, Deputy Speaker's Office, New York State Assembly

Thomas J. Malesky, Chief, Bureau of Educational Finance Research, New York State Education Department

John J. Marchi, Chairman, Finance Committee, New York State Senate

Frank J. Mauro, Secretary, Ways and Means Committee, New York State Assembly

Francis J. O'Connor, Director, Division of Educational Finance, New York State Education Department

Vel Pillai, Sr., Budget Examiner, New York State Division of the Budget

David Porter, Dean, School of Business and Public Administration, California State University, San Bernardino

Claudio R. Prieto, Assistant to the Commissioner for Policy Analysis, Office of Program Planning and Evaluation, New York State Education Department

James R. Ruhl, Assistant Program Secretary to the Majority, New York State Senate

Peter D. Salins, Chairman, Department of Urban Affairs, Hunter College, City University of New York

Richard J. Sauer, Associate Commissioner for Administrative Services, New York State Education Department

Joan Scheuer, Consultant to the Deputy Chancellor, New York City Board of Education

Jose Serrano, Chairman, Education Committee, New York State Assembly

Leonard P. Stavisky, Ranking Minority Member, Education Committee, New York State Senate

Daniel B. Walsh, Majority Leader, New York State Assembly

David C. Warner, Professor, Lyndon Johnson School of Public Affairs, University of Texas at Austin

Lois J. Wilson, Administrator, School Finance Services, New York State School Boards Association

In addition, we wish to thank our friends and associates who have unstintingly given of their time and professional competence in providing research, technical, and secretarial assistance and who have read and commented on the manuscript.

Virginia P. Albert	Susan Graham
Randall G. Bluth	Karen R. Kaufmann
Ann S. Coates	Donald M. Marilla
Barbara Cohen	Judith Schuchalter
Mark F. Glaser	Elizabeth B. Sommers
Albert Gordon	

Without the invaluable assistance of all the foregoing, this book would not exist. Obviously, we are solely responsible for all conclusions and any errors of fact.

Edwin Margolis
Stanley Moses

INTRODUCTION

The focus of this book is the struggle to eliminate the significant differences that currently exist in the amount of monies expended for children in different public schools. We seek to explain why it is so difficult to achieve equality of educational opportunity in American society, whether defined in a minimal sense of provision of equal financing, or in a broader sense, the provision of specialized compensatory programs and equal opportunity for all students. Both goals are in fact becoming more distant as financial inequalities are increasing.

It is not our intention to produce a specialized textbook in educational finance, law or the political process. Rather, this book is designed as a primer on the politics of the struggle for equality. It is intended to be read by students, teachers, laymen, educational administrators, school board members, political decision makers and others who influence the political process but do not necessarily have a background in the field of educational finance. Basic literacy in this area for the non-specialist must include exposure to the philosophical, historical, legal and political factors which affect outcomes; we attempt to provide this exposure.

As a consequence of this approach and our experience in the legislative area, we have developed an explanation for the fact that, after more than a century of effort by reformers, equality of fiscal inputs has not been achieved and is in fact becoming more distant. We focus upon the complex array of cultural, social, economic, political and legal factors which account for this phenomenon, and in particular why it is that traditional attempts at reform have failed to reach their goal.

Our second major objective is to influence professors in school

1

finance courses throughout the nation to reduce the tendency to emphasize theoretical goals without sufficiently examining the political forces which control outcomes. Although our analysis of the failure to reach equality focuses on the dynamics of New York State legislative politics, the book has important implications for scholars nationally.

We present a critique of the traditional orientation of educators and reformers to concentrate on theoretical constructs of educational aid formulas as the major vehicle for reform, thereby falling into a major conceptual trap. Reformers, and also many academics who teach the subject in schools of education, focus upon the formula as the key element in the reform process, ignoring the fact that it is the political process that determines the outcomes. We argue that the real determinant of the mathematical output of the formula is not the elements of the formula itself, but rather the political forces which direct the formula towards predetermined results. We therefore hope that this book will also be used as a supplemental text in school finance and politics of education courses.

The first chapter concentrates on the ideal of equal educational opportunity as a central part of American democracy. Issues of educational policy have become increasingly important because of the role played by schools in modern society, and because of the increased involvement of government both in formulating educational policies that determine the distribution of access to education and in affecting the quality of education that is made available. This has resulted in increasing political conflict regarding educational policy, as different groups struggle to preserve or increase their access to educational resources, and has heightened debate on the question of the standard that should guide formulation and implementation of educational policy.

Chapter 2 traces the more-than-century-long struggle for equality in New York State that has dominated the attention of local and state government, the judicial and legislative branches, and educational administrators and reformers. Their prime goal has been the creation of a system of educational finance that would eliminate the fiscal input disparities that exist as a result of inequalities among school districts in per-pupil wealth. Since the system in New York State still clearly reflects a high degree of inequality, we shall describe the long and tortuous history of the, at best, only partially successful attempts to remedy this situation.

Chapter 3 analyzes the institutional and political constraints, those forces of power and politics that have prevented the success of equalization efforts, even when these efforts seemed to have the support of a broad-based constituency. Our focus will be on the dynamics of the legislative process in New York State and why the interplay of coalitions, parties and conference majorities leads to agreements that of necessity do not result in a significant lessening of educational inequalities.

Growing disenchantment with the political process after years of effort to achieve change prompted reformers across the nation and in New York State to mount legal challenges to existing systems of educational finance, claiming violations both of fundamental federal and state constitutional rights and of state statutes. The fourth chapter traces the issues involved and the outcomes resulting from attempts to impose through the courts changes that could not be achieved through the political and legislative processes. Our concern shall be with trial developments throughout the nation as well as with the specific drama of the *Levittown v. Nyquist* case, a confrontation that dominated the attention of New York State policy makers during the drawn-out process of judicial decision making that began in 1974 and was finally resolved in June of 1982. This chapter concludes with a discussion of newly articulated constitutional constructs of "minimally adequate education" which may reopen closed judicial doors.

Chapter 5 updates our analysis of New York State to reflect the current post-*Levittown* situation—that is, conditions that now prevail as a result of the decision by the state's highest court, the Court of Appeals, upholding the legality of the current system of educational finance. The current fiscal and budgetary situation in New York State is assessed as well as the anticipated effects on educational inequality now and in the future.

Chapter 6 assesses certain basic characteristics of society and the governmental system that have precluded success in achieving equality, and why it is that, after a century of concerted effort, fiscal equalization is now less probable than it has been in a long time. We shall reflect on those basic beliefs, values and practices that have played a major role in this process, and also what we learn from this process about the functioning of American society. We conclude that the current system of education finance results in neither equity nor equality in the treatment of school children and that, given the interests and conflicts involved, society and government are not able to attain such a goal.

A number of difficult and unsettling questions are presented to us as we ponder the limitations and inadequacies involved in our approach to this subject. We proceed to discuss them, not with the thought that we can dispose of them, but hopefully with the aim of reducing some of their potency, enabling us to proceed directly to the task at hand.

An initial hesitancy on our part related to limitations inherent in the development of the case study approach, especially since our major interests and concerns are with national and intergovernmental policy issues. We decided to emphasize New York because we believe that New York's importance goes beyond that of a single state. We refer not only to its size but its significance as the fount of the development of education finance theory. This role was enhanced by the pioneer work done at Teachers College at Columbia University in providing leadership for a cadre of thinkers and doers who first shaped the New York system and then went on to implement their views in other states and nations. The struggle for educational opportunity has been a central part of the state's history, probably more prominent than in most. Its development relates to many other states and to American society in general.

There exist important questions regarding relationships among educational inputs and outputs, learning and the educational system, and also regarding the concentration upon money as the measure of educational opportunity and equality. Neither of the authors believes there is a clear relationship of financial inputs to educational outputs, to student achievement in school and in test scores or to educational outcomes, and the subsequent effects of education upon the student's occupation, income and personal satisfactions. Increased monies may make a difference, but in our view they are not clearly the critical and determining differences in these matters.

Our views on the subject might best be summed up as the belief that money does make a difference, especially to the physical environment of education. But the evidence is conflicting as to whether this will result in significant improvement of educational outputs, or perhaps even more important, of other subsequent lifetime outcomes.

We also believe that a real test of the effectiveness of money has not been made, either in the amounts of resources committed or in the duration of the commitment. The evidence is still not conclusive on this very important issue of social policy. Perhaps if the issue were pursued in a serious manner, we might get a real test of the effectiveness of the kind of equity-oriented policies represented in Kern Alexander's equity hierarchy, discussed in Chapter 1. But since this approach is unlikely to occur in the foreseeable future, we must content ourselves more with hunches than with clear evidence. And our hunch is that money does matter, up to a point; but there are other things that are probably at least as important, such as family circumstances, educational leadership, cultural differences and teacher morale.

We also recognize the dangers of an approach to educational policy that focuses solely on children in schools. Learning and personal development involve for all children experiences far more diverse than those provided by enclosure within the confines of school buildings with established curriculums. Learning is far too important and serious a business to be restricted solely to the activities of professional educators and schools. Attempts to improve education must involve attention to the whole range of cultural and environmental influences that affect children. It is especially important in responding to the needs of those who come from poor and disadvantaged backgrounds that fail to provide many of the opportunities available to children from more affluent homes.

We believe that our focus on financial inputs is especially helpful in enabling us to understand American society and government. Dollars are a clearly distinguishable index of power and privilege, most intensely pursued as a desirable good. It is assumed that more money is better than less, and that in education, as in most matters, the expenditure of more money assures greater quality. Educational expenditures are also generally viewed as an indicator of educational quality and community concern and involvement. Parents generally desire more expenditures for schools, especially when the bill is paid by others. And most parental groups, educational organizations and local communities that are involved with education attempt to secure the highest possible level of funding through organized pressure at the local, state and sometimes even national levels. Success or failure at mobilizing resources is seen as evidence of their political influence and power.

Regardless of how money actually affects the quality of education, it is still extremely important because so many believe it does have such an effect and attach significance to levels of educational allocations as being an indicator of the successful use of political power. Consequently, when we study educational finance, we are able to observe the impact of values and power on decision making in an environment of intense competition and conflict for limited resources. In this context, issues of educational finance are important, even if their impact is not clearly related to effects on the educational process itself. In analyzing the struggle over distribution of resources, we therefore better understand how society and government work and also why it is that the goal of equality is so elusive and the efforts of reformers are usually doomed to failure.

For purposes of this study we cut across many disciplinary domains, occasionally bypassing issues that by themselves would merit far greater attention. This may upset other toilers within these academic specializations. The literature on education and public finance attests to the development of many subdisciplines related to issues in political science, philosophy, history, law, economics and public administration. In this book, we work our way gingerly across this terrain, poaching and learning wherever we can. If the disciplinary boundaries seem blurred, we believe this is due to the nature of the subject. We hope that this book will make an important contribution by developing an inter-disciplinary perspective on a field where concentration on specializations often limits comprehensive understanding.

We also had more personal determinants for our choice of this approach. Judge Edwin Margolis has worked for more than a quarter of a century in the executive, legislative and judicial branches of federal, state and local governments, and has been privileged thereby to learn much about the operations of politics and policy. His legal background has facilitated an understanding of the relationships among politics, law, government and administration—complexities that are especially prevalent in the governance of education.

Co-author, Professor Stanley Moses, has been a colleague of Judge Margolis in the Urban Planning Graduate Program at Hunter College of the City University of New York, and also has an extensive background in the study and practice of educational policy in federal, state and local governments. These experiences have been especially enlivened by being witness to the odysseys of two sons making their way through the privileged habitat of an affluent suburban school district.

Issues related to educational policy are a fascinating subject for study and we have both been challenged in many ways. We hope that we have been able to impart some of the stimulation and excitement that we have experienced in studying this subject. We also hope that this book contributes to a greater understanding of critical issues involved in educational finance.

1.

THE CONCEPT AND IDEAL OF EQUAL EDUCATIONAL OPPORTUNITY

The history of education since the industrial revolution shows a continual struggle between two forces: the desire by members of society to have educational opportunity for all and the desire of each family to provide the best education it can provide for its own children. Neither of these desires is to be despised; they both lead to investment by the older generation in the younger. But they can lead to quite different concrete actions.

  —James S. Coleman, *Private Wealth and Public Education*

* * *

Underlying this dilemma is a basic question: What do equity and justice require of the state in providing for a system of education? Does equity require that the fiscal capacity of units of government be equalized in order that all students may have equal access to educational fiscal resources? Does equity require that the state fiscally supplement the educational program of each individual in such a way as to compensate for mental, physical, cultural, social and economic conditions which may place an individual at an educational disadvantage in the educational process? To answer these questions requires a philosophical definition of equity, a legal definition of equity, a

7

review of the status of school finance equity, and finally an application of the concept of equity to practice.

> —Kern Alexander, "Concepts of Equity" in
> *Financing Education*

Ideals regarding equity and justice are at the center of political conflict in democratic societies, having a strong influence on the determination of public policy. The manner in which they are defined sets standards that determine the allocation of resources for different purposes and needs. Even if ideals of equity and justice do not reflect reality and there is a general consensus that they are impracticable, they nevertheless exercise strong influence upon values and behavior. This is because the struggle for greater justice and equity is a continuing part of the political process, carried on within and between the generations, never really fully resolved and always certain to reappear in one form or another.

We are concerned in this book with the specific issue of equality of educational opportunity, a subject that has exercised the thought and imagination of policy makers since the beginning of public administration in this country. The dynamics of the struggle for equal opportunity in public schools may be observed from the beginning of the republic when education first became a major activity of state and local government. Even then, with the creation of one-room school houses within walking distance of each child, there was recognition of the need for a state role in providing for educational opportunity.

In all modern industrialized societies, the school system is a major determinant of status and occupational differentiation and the place of pre-labor force socialization and training. Education has increasingly become the major vehicle for economic and social mobility as different groups strive to improve their situation. This has resulted in the development of a mass system of universal schooling which has increased the educational attainment of the population. The American educational system is also a major arena for conflicts involving the distribution of public resources as well as for competition among individuals and groups for preferred treatment.

Two major problems are perceived as undesirable aspects of the American educational system. The first is the quality of schooling that is reflected in disaffection and high dropout rates, especially among inner-city minority students. The inability of dropouts to be absorbed into society, their high rates of unemployment, poverty, addiction and crime, are sources of social concern and dissatisfaction with the performance of the school system.

The second problem is the great inequalities in expenditures per pupil, even among students living within the same geographic area. While this book deals with the latter issue of educational opportunity in the financial sense, we believe that there probably is a relationship, at least at some level, between the availability of resources and the quality of education, although this connection has not been sufficiently demonstrated by empirical research. However, it does seem clear that a 15 to 1 teacher-pupil teacher ratio is more stimulative of learning than a 30 to 1 ratio.

We believe that the inadequacy and inequality of expenditures available for the schooling of children are important factors in the denial of educational opportunity to millions of American youngsters. Furthermore, these disparities are inextricably related to the unique structure of educational governance in the United States.

Structural Determinants

A unique characteristic of the American educational system is the existence of a state-local system of planning and control of education, with the responsibility for educational governance lodged at the state level in association with a system of independent local school district governance. In 1987-88, 15,577 school districts were reported[1] as having responsibility for administering elementary and secondary education, planning budgets subject to voter approval and raising revenue through local property taxes. State aid is relied on to supplement school property taxes that are raised locally.

There are differences among the various states as to the distribution of educational responsibilities between local and state governments. Table 1 (see Statistical Appendix) depicts the sharing of total educational costs among local, state and federal governments. The portion of state contributions has risen in recent years, amounting to 49.8 percent of total revenues in 1986-87. Federal support, which had risen significantly in the 1960s, primarily as a result of Great Society legislation, has declined in the last few years—from 9.8 percent of total public elementary and secondary school revenues in 1979-80, to 6.4 percent in 1986-87.

Table 2 in the Statistical Appendix depicts the sources of New York State educational revenues for the periods between 1972 to 1973 and 1989 to 1990. This reflects a fairly stable relationship among the different shares—federal, state and local—during this period and a somewhat greater reliance on the local share, in comparison to the national average of most other states. (See Table 3 in Statistical Appendix.) The historically greater dependence upon local sources of revenue for the support of education in New York State results in a system more resistant to reform efforts seeking fiscal equalization than would otherwise be the case and is a subject that will be referred to later in this book.

American emphasis on special treatment for education results from a strong antipathy to central government and a belief that education should be subject to local control. This has resulted in the establishment of education as a separate governmental function with a fiscal integrity of its own, reflecting the view that education is not "political" and should be divorced from a budgetary process involving competition with other activities of government.

The roots of the American system of educational governance can be traced to the U.S. Constitution. Education was not delegated to the federal government and therefore was reserved to the individual states, which in turn apportioned areas for creation of an independent school district form of governance. The different state patterns of local control then developed gradually over the next two hundred years. While state governments now direct and control much of education, including curriculum requirements, in a centralized manner (and also contribute the major portion of its revenue), the general perception nevertheless remains one of independent governance, fiscal autonomy and local control.

The dependence of education on resources tied to local property values has resulted in great disparities in the abilities of school districts to finance themselves. At an earlier time, this was reflected in the differences between rural and urban areas, with cities having a favored position due to the wealth of their newly developed central business districts as contrasted with the lower property values of rural areas. More recently, there has been concern with the disparities between more affluent suburban school districts and less advantaged central city and rural areas.

In response to these structural determinants of fiscal inequality, state governments have regularly sought to compensate for resource differences at the local level by developing equalizing operating-aid formulas that would distribute monies in an inverse relationship to local per-pupil property wealth. While the state goal was usually not full equalization and the elimination of all differences in per-pupil expenditures, there has been an attempt to provide resources that would ensure at least a foundation for a minimally adequate schooling for all children. However, since each school district determines its own local share, great fiscal inequalities have always existed among school districts in most of the states.

Disparities and inequalities in resources and expenditures can be reduced or eliminated in any one of the following five ways: by far greater tax burdens on property owners in poorer areas, by enlarging the geographic areas of the school district, by turning to either the state or federal governments for both more monies and greater attention to equalization, by limiting the authority of wealthy districts to raise revenues, or by introducing state responsibility for total funding of public elementary and secondary schools. Essentially all proposals for education finance reform involve any one or a combination of these approaches.

This book describes the history and dynamics of the struggle for educational opportunity in New York State. Before proceeding, however, it will be helpful to acquaint the reader with a rudimentary understanding of theoretical and philosophical approaches to concepts and goals of equity and equality and the manner in which they influence policies related to educational opportunity. First, we shall discuss questions regarding the appropriate focus of study for measuring educational performance. Then we shall consider different conceptual definitions of equity and equality and the policies to which they lead. We shall then examine a new development in educational philosophy, also a source of current court challenges, that proposes an alternative approach to equality of educational opportunity—the concept of educational adequacy.

The Problem of the Measure

Thus a concept of equality of opportunity which focused on *effects* of schooling began to take form. The actual decision of the Court [*Brown v. Board of Education*] was in fact a confusion of two unrelated premises: this new concept which looked at results of schooling, and the legal premise that the use of race as a basis for school assignment violates fundamental freedoms. But what is important for the evolution of the concept of equality of opportunity is that a new and different assumption was introduced, the assumption that equality of opportunity depends in some fashion upon effects of schooling . . . by introducing the question of effects of schooling, the Court brought into the open the implicit goals of equality of educational opportunity—that is, goals having to do with the *results* of school—to which the original concept was somewhat awkwardly directed.[2]

Problems unique to educational finance complicate issues of policy formulation in a manner not resolved by grand pronouncements of the ideals of equality. Some of the problems involve determination of an ideal standard of justice that is to serve as a guide to public policy formulation. Other problems arise from disagreements over the effects of such policies. Depending on the purposes being pursued, one might focus on questions related to access, to inputs, to the process itself, to the immediate outputs or to long-term consequences and outcomes.

Access refers to the availability of opportunities for participation without restrictions based upon sex, religion, race or other factors that violate the fundamental rights of individuals. Inputs involve the amount of dollars available for capital and current costs. Process refers to the content of educational services. Outputs refer to a variety of behavioral measures related to student achievement that may include test scores, promotion, school completion and special forms of distinction. Outcomes refer to the subsequent lifetime experiences of those who pass through the educational system, the implicit assumption being that there is a direct connection between schooling and subsequent occupation, income level and general satisfaction.

The particular focus that is chosen leads to different measures of assessment as well as different policy implications. It also reflects the value biases and interests of the observer. Depending on one's values and political orientation, one could conclude that equality of educational opportunity was achieved in relation to any one of these measures, or that it was not realizable unless and until inequalities had been eliminated in all of these areas.

In its more limited sense, equality of educational opportunity might refer solely to the development of universal access to elementary and secondary education, seen simply as the provision of an opportunity. In its more idealistic and ambitious sense, it might be defined as the achievement of an optimal state where individual differences in educational achievement reflect only innate characteristics of students and not the effects of class, racial, geographic or other factors related to the backgrounds of students. Belief in the latter orientation would lead to the advocacy of policies to compensate for and eliminate educational results that are caused by such differences, an outlook embodied in compensatory education programs. This would result in policies far different from those based on the view that equality of educational opportunity should be defined as sameness of treatment for all, a point of view that underlies the advocacy of fiscal equalization. We now proceed to a consideration of these contrasting approaches to equity and how they might lead to the formulation of opposing policies affecting equality of educational opportunity.

Values and Policies

Herein lies the essential difference between the educational finance definition of mere equality and a more pervasive standard of equity. A system of educational finance which merely equalizes, or neutralizes, or provides equal distribution to local school districts with low fiscal capacity is admittedly inferior, on this scale of social justice, to a system which attempts to fully fiscally equalize and, in addition, to provide resources to the "least-favored" children in the Rawlsian tradition.

... Their [the plaintiffs] concept of equity is that the state must (1) erase the fiscal disparities among school districts, (2) correct with cost differential programs for variations in educational needs, and (3) require a uniform local effort at a level high enough to assure adequate resources in every school district.[3]

* * *

Choices must be made about the groups of concern—children and taxpayers, the legitimate and illegitimate distinctions among them, the objects of concern, the equity principles to be applied and statistical measures of these principles.... All of these have to be addressed by governors, legislators, and educators as school finance policies are forged. Many choices are primarily value judgments, while others can be made based on careful research and analysis.... Research can inform these choices, but value-laden questions of goals are not appropriate concerns for researchers alone. What research can do is to contribute to the ability of policy makers to measure the alternative equity goals with available data and to evaluate the movement toward or away from them.[4]

Educational policies are outcomes of a historical process of political and social conflict as different groups struggle to achieve policies that will reflect their notions of justice and equity. Conflicts over the allocation and distribution of public monies are at the heart of the budgetary process, a permanent and continual feature involving all levels of government. What distinguishes education from other services is the conflict between the actual fiscal realities and espoused ideals regarding justice and equity. On the one hand, education is universally acknowledged to be a "merit" good which should be made universally available to all children irrespective of their family background and economic circumstances. On the other hand, the governmental organization of education dictates that there will be great differences in the amount of money available for the education of different children, based on where their families reside.

The fact that society assumes the burden of paying for some or all of the education of poor children whose parents cannot afford those costs is accepted as legitimate and desirable, reflecting a responsibility to make available an educational opportunity for all children. But it is far from a commitment to equality of opportunity, even in the minimal sense of making an equal amount of resources available for the education of all children.

There is great conflict about the standard and measure which should be applied in assessing the equity and equality orientation of educational policies. Kern Alexander has developed an "equity hierarchy" which serves as a useful guide to various notions of philosophical equity as applied specifically to educational finance. (See Chart 1.) The aim is to evaluate a given structure of educational finance as to whether it reflects a "higher" or "lower" level of equity. The two extremes are polarized by the contrast between total local control and choice, commutativity and positivism, which compensates for differences in both financial resources and in the educational needs of children.

Commutativity, the least interventionist on the equity hierarchy, calls for no intervention whatsoever in the educational finances of a local school district. The school district is left to its own resources without external assistance. It retains the freedom to choose the tax rate to apply to its real property wealth base. Poor districts can tax themselves as much and the wealthy districts as little as they desire. Commutativity does not actually exist in its purest form inasmuch as it rules out all foundation formula-equalizing aid which, as a matter of fact, does exist to some degree in all states. However, the principle of commutativity is the philosophical basis of opposition to state aid, and also to federal compensatory educational programs.

Equal distribution, which we will refer to in this book as equality, incorporates the principle of fiscal neutrality, while at the same time allowing commutative aspects of local choice. Fiscal neutrality is essentially a negative principle that posits a limited notion of equity. It asserts that the amount of resources available for a child's education should not be a function of the property wealth available in a local school district. It commits the state to policies which guarantee that an equal level of tax effort will result in the same amount of revenue per pupil. An equal fiscal base, full fiscal equalization, is thereby provided for all school districts, regardless of property wealth, income levels or geographic location.

School finance formulas, involving techniques of district power equalization, implement the objectives of fiscal neutrality. This involves guaranteeing that the poorest district will at a predetermined base level have available to it the same resources as the richest district. At the same time, local choice allows districts to choose to tax themselves at levels that will generate more revenue. This accounts for the partiality and limitedness of fiscal neutrality as a standard of equality or equity, since it still allows for the existence of great differences among school districts in revenues raised, and usually results in unequal distribution.

Restitution, the next level on the equity hierarchy, maintains the principle of fiscal neutrality, while including attention to deficiencies caused by social and economic conditions at the local level that result in interdistrict inequality. These conditions refer solely to structural lacks and do not relate to particular needs of students. Restitution accounts for differences related to dissimilar local tax effort, variations in local costs of education, economies of scale and also different kinds of governmental overburdens. Advocates of restitution assert that it is the responsibility of the state to compensate for inter-school district inequalities and disparities. However, by focusing solely upon institutional and structural characteristics, it fails to incorporate standards of equity that will pay attention to differences in student needs and abilities. It is this lack that distinguishes restitution from the highest level of equity—"positivism."

Equality implies the goal of sameness of treatment for all, regardless of their condition, implying that goals of equity have been achieved once this state has been reached. Positivism includes all that has come before but adds a consideration of student needs that may require special programs and more resources. This implies an equity standard that goes beyond simply developing tools that will provide equality, and leads to far more ambitious, complex and uncharted agenda. Ambitious, because it involves circumventing the system of interests and privileges that establish limits to social change; complex, because it involves the testing and development of a set of policy initiatives that imply all sorts of input-output relationships that are as of yet uncertain and unverified; and uncharted, because the dimensions of expenditure, attention and effort that would be required to achieve the goals of equity are unknown and unclear.

There are great disputes regarding an appropriate role for governmental intervention and the desired level of redistributive activities. This debate is carried on in all areas of public policy, education being but a particularly important example of the larger discussion. At one extreme is the notion, posited most aptly by Rawls in his "difference principle," that wealth should be redistributed so as to maximize the position of the least advantaged social and economic class.[5] Hayek's opposing view contends that if outcomes of the marketplace reflect appropriate rewards, redistributive interventions by government have no justification in either political philosophy or in ethical notions of equity.[6] These contrasting orientations provide the rationale for differing policy responses to the educational needs of children.

Normative views are developed as a branch of political philosophy and reflect ideals, values and philosophies of justice and ethics rather than a calculated and pragmatic estimate of the possibilities of the political process. While concepts and values on justice and equity influence the nature and extent of redistribution that should be sought by the state, it is the existing structure of political power and decision making that determines which views are implemented.

A commitment to full equity has never been really tried in this country, the aborted efforts of the Great Society being at best a partial and brief approach. The positivistic standard of equity calls for attention to the specific and unique educational needs of different children. It would require attention to issues related to process and outputs, rather than the mere equalization of fiscal inputs for all school districts. It embodies a more lofty notion of justice that would justify increased intervention to assure that the most disadvantaged—those who have the least and need the most—would receive the greatest level of attention. This is contrary to the situation existing in educational finance in this country, where those who are most privileged through conditions of economic and educational backgrounds generally receive the most attention in terms of the quantity and quality of educational resources made available.

The Search for a New Standard

Again, the key element is that every child is to have access to equal educational opportunity, but that communities are to be free to offer particularly rich and costly educational programs. The foundation program is predicated on the belief that the state is responsible for guaranteeing a minimum of educational resources to each student.

In the foundation program approach, adequacy is the politically determined minimum amount of resources. The idea of educational adequacy is a challenge to the notion that adequacy should be determined by reference to resource inputs. Educational adequacy directs attention to educational outcomes. . . .[7]

The major focus of this book is on the more limited concept of equality—the goal of equalization of fiscal inputs. But before proceeding to this subject, it is necessary to introduce and explain yet another concept: the idea of "educational adequacy." The importance of this idea will be seen more clearly in Chapter 4, where the argument is made that court responses to legal challenges regarding equality of educational opportunity have resulted in the evolution of a new approach to educational policy, the more limited and modest goal of adequacy.

The concept of educational adequacy has recently received attention by those seeking to develop a new goal for educational finance as a result of declining prospects for the realization of more ambitious equity goals. The U.S. Supreme Court has spoken negatively with respect to a federal constitutional mandate for fiscal neutrality. Enthusiasm has dissipated regarding prospects for either successful challenges or subsequent implementation of change by state judiciary systems. And there has been a significant shift in societal support away from interventionist, redistributive educational policies. As a consequence, the energies of many reformers have shifted to the development of a strategy that will lead to the guarantee of a basic minimum level of education for all children, irrespective of differences in individual backgrounds.

In one sense, the approach to adequacy is very similar to the foundation aid programs that are at the heart of educational finance systems developed in this country since the 1920s. It involves a commitment to ensure a minimum level of education for all children. However, the traditional foundation program sought to do this by guaranteeing a basic level of fiscal support for all school districts. This was stated as the responsibility of state government and it was assumed that once resources had been made available by the state to lessen some of the truly gross disparities that existed as a result of local wealth differences, that responsibility was fulfilled. The assumption was that the extra resources in themselves served as the guarantee of a basic minimum level of adequacy for all students.

The difference with adequacy advocates of today is that the emphasis is not upon resources but rather a specified set of educational outcomes—i.e., levels of achievement in reading, writing and mathematics which will serve as the standard for the measurement and determination of adequacy. In the fiscal sense, adequacy represents a lesser commitment to equality for it is not concerned with the equalization of fiscal inputs, only with the assessment and guarantee of educational outcomes.

The centerpiece of this effort involves the specification of just what is involved in the provision of an adequate education. This may involve the consideration and development of output measures for such goals as literacy, mathematics, self-knowledge, civics, work-training, recreational pursuits, creative arts and social ethics. At a more general level, adequacy goals are often defined in terms of "the provision of educational opportunity which is needed in the contemporary setting to equip a child for his role as a citizen and a competitor in the labor market."[8]

The fact that many court and legislative battles are currently being waged over this issue is an indication of the difficulty of such a task. Of course, the formulation of appropriate and desired outcomes will have an important effect on the determination of the required level of fiscal inputs. In that way, the focus on adequacy may become a new cutting edge of reform, albeit through the back door, that leads eventually to more funds for education and also to greater equalization. But current discussions about adequacy are mired in research studies and legal arguments about the specific components of what constitutes an adequate education, a subject discussed more fully in Chapter 4. Consequently, the concept of adequacy is far from becoming an effective force in the determination of educational policy.

Changing Prospects

Our ideals may clash in at least three ways. First, there are conflicts inherent in their meaning, and secondly, those arising from the presence of different levels of social aggregation. Finally, there are conflicts of implementation, those resulting from our choice of tools in making our ideals actual. These three modes of conflict do much to account for the difficulties inherent in attempts to secure equity, excellence, and equality through public policy.[9]

Leaving aside for the moment questions of ideals and ultimate values, we confront an alarming reality in contemporary America. The general public may be antagonistic to redistributive compensatory educational policies because they violate conceptions of the social order. However, far fewer Americans would object to the idea that all children are entitled to equal treatment in the provision of public education. Even those who enjoy a privileged status under the current system of educational governance are constrained in their defense of the status quo. This is because the existing system of inequalities and disparities in the treatment of school children is perceived to be unfair and violative of basic social standards of morality and justice.

It is clear that in most of the states, certainly including New York, great inequalities exist in the distribution of educational resources among different local school districts. Intensely competing interests are involved in the struggle for local, state and federal resources. Involvement is especially great because education is the public service that affects the greatest number of people, represents the largest outlay of public funds and is viewed as having the greatest impact on the well-being of individuals and the larger society.

The 1960s and the period since have exhibited a major shift in the climate of public opinion, clearly reflected in changing attitudes about a broad range of social issues as well as the appropriate role for government. The "War on Poverty" and "Great Society" programs of the 1960s called for major commitments of funds for raising the quality of life of poor people. In many areas—housing, health, employment, public assistance and education—monies were allocated with the expressly stated purpose of advancing most the interests of those who have the least. This was justified on the basis of liberal values which imbued public policies with a redistributive orientation, as well as a Realpolitik response to politically threatening developments occurring among nonwhite and other minority groups concentrated in the large central cities of metropolitan America.

Policy developments in education during this period especially reflect these changes. Historically, there has always been a commitment by state governments to redress at least some of the disparities based upon property wealth differences among the school districts. During the 1960s, programs were developed by the federal government for the first time to make monies available for programs of compensatory education for those most in need. Although these programs were never expanded to the levels originally projected, they nevertheless represented a major federal initiative, with more affluent school districts getting less or sometimes even nothing while poorer districts received the bulk of additional new resources.

It is only during the last few years that we have seen a dramatic shift in the orientation of social policy in the United States. Without evaluating nuances regarding the extent of the conservative tide, it is clear that since the late 1970s, the latter part of President Carter's term, there has been a major attempt to first halt the expansion and then to reduce the variety and costs of these programs.

As a result, federal programs of compensatory education for poor children and inner-city minority groups have been significantly reduced. Resistance to increases in school district taxes have once more forced poor districts to rely on increased state aid. But, the very factors which have generated increased opposition to government spending for social programs at the federal level are also likely to limit the responsiveness of state governments to the special needs of poorer school districts.

All these changes have had an important effect on the current condition of equality of educational opportunity. Shifts and swings in the political mood are part of the long history of the struggle. In this book, we shall focus on only one aspect of that struggle—the allocation of financial resources. In Chapter 2, we shall analyze developments in New York State during a two-century effort to expand educational opportunity by state intervention to equalize monies available to local school districts.

NOTES

1. National Center for Education Statistics, U.S. Department of Education, *Digest of Educational Statistics 1989* (Washington, DC: USDA, 1989), Table 80, p. 90.
2. James S. Coleman, "The Concept of Equality of Educational Opportunity," *Equal Educational Opportunity* (Cambridge, MA: Harvard University Press, 1969), p. 17.
3. Kern Alexander, "Concepts of Equity," *Financing Education: Overcoming Inefficiency and Inequity,* Walter W. McMahon and Terry G. Geske, eds. (Urbana: University of Illinois Press, 1982), pp. 201-202.
4. Allan Odden, et. al., *Equity in School Finance, Report No. F79-9* (Denver, CO: Education Finance Center, October 1979), p. 17.
5. John Rawls, *A Theory of Justice* (Cambridge, MA: Harvard University Press, 1971), pp. 75-78.
6. F. A. Hayek, *Law, Legislation and Liberty,* 3 Vols. (Chicago: University of Chicago Press, 1973-1979).
7. Arthur E. Wise, "Educational Adequacy: A Concept in Search of Meaning," *Journal of Educational Finance* 8 (Winter 1983), p. 309.
8. Ibid., p. 301.
9. Thomas F. Green, "Excellence, Equity, and Equality," in *Handbook of Teaching and Policy*, L. Shulman and A. Syliss, eds. (New York: Longman, 1983), p. 318.

2.
FINANCING SCHOOL CHILDREN IN NEW YORK STATE

> To inquire into the best form of government in the abstract (as it is called) is not a chimerical, but a highly practical employment of scientific intellect; and to introduce into any country the best institutions which, in the existing state of that country, are capable of in any tolerable degree fulfilling the conditions, is one of the most rational objects to which practical effort can address itself.
>
> —John Stuart Mill

In this chapter, we shall trace the history of educational finance in New York State with special attention to the manner in which a state and local partnership has been developed in the planning and implementation of free public education. We shall look at major problems that have hindered development of universal access to education and equality of educational opportunity. This will involve consideration of several factors. These include the governance of education, the emphasis on local control, the system of educational finance that causes inequalities in per-pupil expenditures resulting from differences in local per-pupil property values, and the ineffectiveness of the state aid equalizing formula in compensating for local property wealth disparities and different student needs. Those factors of power and politics involved in the legislative process itself that serve to preserve the existing status of inequality will be mentioned, then explored in depth in Chapter 3.

The Early State Role

The first duty of government and the surest evidence of good government is the encouragement of education.[1]

* * *

The legislature shall provide for the maintenance and support of a system of free common schools, wherein all the children of this state may be educated.[2]

The concern of government with the educational needs of children has been a very early part of New York State history, pre-dating even the American Revolution. Two major concerns have been at the heart of its development and have often resulted in conflicting goals and activities—free public education and equality of educational opportunity. From the onset, educators realized there was a need for some form of state involvement, at least in stimulating the development of public educational opportunities for all children. At the same time, there was concern with great income and property wealth differences which made it clear that the majority of children would never be able to afford school—let alone any degree of educational quality—unless public policy made free public education available to all.

The issue of wealth differences among areas was also of concern. As long as localities were to be responsible for the financing of education, it was clear that the state must intervene in some way to mitigate the extreme wealth differences that existed among areas of the state and especially between urban and rural areas.

These two goals—free public education and the lessening of the direct relationship between wealth and public educational opportunity—remain among the prime concerns that dominate educational policy to this very day. Defining a suitable role for governmental intervention in order to offset inequalities related to variations in local property wealth remains a matter of intense conflict, reaching across all areas of the state and affecting children, families and the local communities. How much education should be made available at what cost and to whom? What level of state intervention should be developed to allocate resources to families or areas that would not by themselves be able to ensure a minimal level of opportunity for all children?

Prior to the initial state aid venture of 1795, education in New York State was available most often to the children of the well-to-do, through a system of parochial elementary schools established first by the Dutch

Reformed Church and then by the Church of England.[3] Students paid tuition, with the exception of those who were verified as eligible paupers. Some state funds were made available to the New York State Board of Regents, established in 1784, which distributed them to private academies.

In 1795, the New York State Legislature first began to supply regular appropriations for the support of public education. It allocated £20,000 a year (the equivalent of $50,000 at that time) for five years for "the purpose of encouraging and maintaining schools in the several cities and towns in this state."[4] The aid was to be distributed among all the counties of the state on the basis of population in proportion to the number of electors for members of the New York State Assembly in each county. Localities were required to levy a school tax sufficient to raise a sum equal to one-half of the state aid.

The first attempt at state aid soon met its demise. Many localities refused to levy the local educational tax, and when at the end of the five-year period only three-fifths of the allocated money was actually spent, it was decided to terminate the aid program. This early attempt requiring local matching funds demonstrated the inability or unwillingness of local areas to tax specifically for public educational needs.

The passage of the Common School Act of 1812 represented a major expansion of the state role in planning and supporting the concept of public education. Chapter 242 of the laws of 1812 divided existing towns of the state into school districts, and established provisions for the creation of new counties and towns. A State Superintendent of Instruction was appointed to supervise the disbursement of school funds to counties on a population basis. Within counties, towns were designated both as the recipient and administrator, and they also had responsibility for levying a local tax at least equal to state aid. Since towns were allowed to raise up to twice the amount of state aid, this system relied upon local choice to determine the amount of their levy.

These developments represent the first institutionalization of school governance, which led to the reliance upon local property wealth for the funding of education—the source of the inequality which persists to this day. The basic elements of inequality were now in place—the dependence upon the wealth and will of local districts to supplement state school aid, and the delineation of towns as areas to be divided into self-contained school districts. By 1840, there were over 10,000 school districts and the number rose to 11,870 in 1868.[5] The number remained over 10,000 until 1925, when laws promoting consolidation were passed. Given these two basic elements of fragmented governmental authority for education along with disparate wealth resources among local areas, the inevitability of the current situation one hundred seventy years later seems clear. All that remained was for the subsequent impacts of industrialism, urbanization and suburbanization to determine our contemporary reality.

The major issue which dominated the rest of the nineteenth century was tuition and the struggle for a system of free public education. The Common School Act of 1812 and subsequent reenactments assumed the payment of tuition or "rate bills" to supplement state and town appropriations. Parents who were certified as paupers were exempt from paying tuition. However, since many parents refused to apply for certification as paupers most children of the poor did not attend school. This situation provided added stimulus for the free school movement, a goal which required the rest of the nineteenth century to achieve.

Various attempts were made to secure free public education. Laws were enacted, referenda passed and arrangements devised between the state, counties, towns and school districts to facilitate that end. But the realities of an agrarian economy took precedence as many citizens refused to pay the tax levies for education. For example in 1849, the vote was 249,872 to 91,951 in favor of a law "establishing free schools throughout the state."[6] But when it came to the task of implementation, practical difficulties seemed to thwart the electoral dictate. The fundamental issue was who should pay? Many counties and towns did not levy the local property taxes necessary to pay their share of school costs. Similarly, newly created school districts chose not to levy new taxes when more established governments refused to do so. Consequently, the length of the school year varied; for most students, no more than the required four-months minimum.

The lack of governmental commitment or ability undermined achieving the goal of the 1849 electoral dictate. State action expanded to take up the slack, primarily by abolition of tuition rate bills. Later that attention focused upon non-financial issues, such as the length of the school day and school year and the educational attainment of the population. However, the primary challenge to state policy in the nineteenth century remained the establishment and implementation of a universal system of public education, the achievement of which was still far away.

The New York State Constitution of 1895 codified the fruits of more than a century of struggle to expand the entitlements of public education. It resolved once and for all the conflict regarding tuition rate fees and the commitment to free public education. Its clause on education stated that "the legislature shall provide for the maintenance and support of a system of free common schools, wherein all the children of this state may be educated."[7]

As long as free public education was dependent upon the good will and cooperation of county, town and local school districts in partnership with the state, that goal could be easily set aside, a casualty of fiscal stringency, along with local antagonisms against supporting public education. Now that the goal was enshrined in the constitution, it became a primary and inviolable guarantee, a compact between the state and its citizens, a symbol of belief in the needs of the young and commitment to the support of education. Universal public education was no longer the issue. The guarantee of universal free access to schools established the precondition necessary for state government to devote attention to issues of equality of educational opportunity.

Fragmentation of School Governance

If school district taxing power is not to be transferred to a unit no smaller than a county, there is no hope at all of finding a workable equalization formula combining state and local support. The only alternative is complete state financing of schools. Aside from taxing power (the key to the difficulty), there is almost no chance that a satisfactory measure of fiscal capacity can be found for school districts.[8]

It is ironic that the two great nineteenth-century legislative accomplishments of the public education movement contributed to both increasing educational opportunities and to inequalities in resources. The Common School Act of 1812, which divided the state into exceedingly small geographic areas and gave those areas administrative functions, provided the precedent for school district taxation. The free school laws of 1849 and 1851, by giving taxing power to school districts, inevitably led to reliance on local school district taxation, which, in effect, mandated resource inequalities.

The structure of school finance combined with the system of fragmented school governance to allow for many school districts of differing size. The existence of many independent school districts with their separate tax bases and taxing powers determines the great disparities that are bound to occur. This dependence on the separate governance system of individual school districts is at the heart of the issue of inequality. Its persistence and resistance to change, often buttressed by an ideology of liberty and local control, have blocked attempts at reform. Reformers who have sought to move the system more toward equality have been rebuked by the power of locally entrenched traditions and interests which seek to maintain the existing system—even though many of these same districts are disadvantaged as a result of their separate governmental status.

School districts are local units of government created by the state to administer education. The school district is an independent unit of government attached to a specific geographic area, often overlapping several towns and villages. In New York State, all school districts, except those of the five largest cities, are designated independent and are empowered to make their own taxing and spending decisions—subject only in the case of city school districts to constitutional tax and debt limits and in the case of all other independent districts to voter approval of the annual budget. The school district is responsible for the elementary and secondary education of all school age children residing within its boundaries.

School districts with high residential value concentrations, or with commercial and industrial centers within their boundaries, are able to generate high revenue with low tax rates. However, property-poor school districts are obliged to tax at much higher rates to achieve the same level of locally generated revenues. This system of school finance is at the heart of contemporary problems of fiscal inequalities, owing its origin to the decision to devise a system of school governance that allows for the fragmentation of school districts without rational consideration of economic resources or educational needs.

The fragmentation of school districts was a result of the limits of transportation in the pre-industrial period. The requirement that schools be within walking distance of all children resulted in a proliferation of independent school districts throughout the state. A basic principle of government organization is that the smaller the administrative unit, the greater the likelihood of a mismatch between available taxable resources and service demands. Larger units make possible greater heterogeneity, while smaller units are more likely to result in homogeneous extremes in terms of both resources and needs.

A major consolidation occurred in 1897 with the five-county reorganization of New York City. This resulted in the merging of 350 independent school districts into a single citywide dependent school district. Since that time, the great wealth of the central borough, Manhattan, has been regularly subsidizing educational and other service needs of the outer boroughs at a level that could not have been achieved within the previously fragmented governmental structure. The benefits of what occurred in 1897 are less evident today at a time when decentralization and suburbanization have resulted in an increasing dispersion of wealth to affluent suburbs outside the jurisdiction of the city. This development would have dismayed the lawmakers of 1897 who thought they were framing boundaries that would forever encompass future regional economic activity.

The Concern for Equality

The designers of the operating aid formula wanted to replace the haphazard political process that determined school aid with a formula built on objective criteria. They wanted their formula to:

- stabilize funding from year to year;

- depoliticize funding;

- base distribution on objective criteria that could be verified;

- equalize aid on the basis of each local district's ability-to-pay and student need;

- retain local control.[9]

Now that the state was to have a major role in guaranteeing free universal public education, attention was given to development of mechanisms that would determine the form of shared state responsibility with local governments. For the first time, in 1902, measures of school district wealth were used in the apportionment of state aid. School districts were aided in inverse relationship to their total assessed valuations. In addition, there was a form of aid known as "stimulation grants," such as supplements allocated in relation to the number of teachers employed. These were precursors to the form of aid that is currently referred to as categorical grants.

These types of aid were adjusted and modified as circumstances changed, and a variety of patchwork arrangements were devised during the next few decades in order to recognize special needs, such as those of immigrant children, the handicapped and illiterates. These were ad hoc, incremental adaptations, lacking as yet any integrated conceptual orientation, either in terms of a total system of state aid, or in terms of the data and information necessary to respond effectively to the needs of an expanding education system.

The creation of an integrated system of educational finance required first the emergence of a philosophical framework that was only then beginning to be developed in universities and state departments of education. The underlying philosophy that was to dominate and form the states' role in education was clearly stated by Professor Ellwood Cubberly in 1905:

> Theoretically, all the children of the state are equally important and are entitled to have the same advantages; practically, this can never be true. The duty of the state is to secure for all as high a minimum of good instruction as is possible, but not to reduce all to this minimum; to place a premium on those local efforts which will enable local communities to rise above the local minimum as far as possible; and to encourage communities to extend their educational energies to new and desirable undertakings.[10]

Professor Cubberly accepted as a given the realities of unequal advantages accruing to children as a result of accidents of birth or other circumstances, such as location. He believed that equalization, in the sense of equality of opportunity for all, is in theory desirable but practically unattainable. Therefore, the state, while seeking to improve conditions in poor districts, must not act to lower the quality of more privileged school districts. Although Cubberly's views provide a basis for compensatory policies of state educational aid, they are far from an aggressive commitment to the pursuit of equal opportunity. He accepts the limits placed in the way of achieving the ideal goals of equality of opportunity, and posits instead a role for government to guarantee a minimum level of adequate education for all children.

The main determinant of state aid in his proposals was the connection between some notion of pupil enrollment in relation to the number of teachers employed. The aim of "stimulation grants" was to reward those districts that developed special educational services by supplementing them with additional monies. Any desired service could be determined as eligible for stimulation aid, and in fact many were. Cubberly was especially concerned with stimulating the expansion of secondary education to the larger population.

The fundamental precepts which have guided and determined state-local relationships in the financing and planning of public education in this nation were developed by Professor Cubberly who was then at Teachers College of Columbia University. His ideas were critical in influencing the views of Robert Haig, George Strayer, Paul Mort, Arvid Burke and others who followed him at Teachers College. They developed the educational aid policies that were subsequently adopted in New York, most other states and in some foreign countries.

In order to develop a rationalized system of state aid, an Educational Finance Inquiry Commission was created in 1921. The major architects of the commission report were Haig and Strayer, who, on assessing New York State educational finance in the 1920s, concluded that, "[a] precise description of the basis upon which federal and state money is apportioned among localities is an elaborate undertaking. The present arrangements are the result of the product of a long history of piecemeal legislation. The result is chaos."[11] They also observed that "[a]pproximately one-half of the state aid is entirely unaffected by the richness of the local economic resources back of the teacher, and the portion which is so affected is allocated in a manner which favors both the very rich and the poor localities at the expense of those which are moderately well off."[12]

The work of this commission provided the framework for the development of a formula-based "foundation program" which would make a prescribed minimum of education available to all students. State aid was to be the difference between (1) the amount raised by the imposition of a hypothetical uniform statewide tax rate on the full value of the real property in each school district, and (2) some state-prescribed minimum yield. Thus, state aid was to be distributed in inverse proportion to local wealth.

Under the original commission concept, the state would calculate the hypothetical uniform tax rate so that when applied to the wealthiest school district, it would generate the precise amount of revenue required to equal the state-determined minimum level educational program. The state would then supplement the difference between the revenue raised by each school district and the wealthiest district at the same tax rate, but only up to this minimum level. And in fact in New York State, this meant that local school districts were free to provide whatever school budget level of expenditures they desired. This enabled wealthy districts to raise large sums of money while taxing at a lower rate than poor districts. This still remains the basic mechanism of the foundation formula concept except that instead of using the wealth base of the richest district, the statewide average district wealth is usually substituted.

Revision of the State Aid Formula

We have a childish faith in "plans." When the inevitable disillusionment comes, we conclude that the "plan" did not work and look for another. In the case of equalization schemes, the disillusionment is prone to come at a time when the original plan has been forgotten and inequality is discovered all over again.[13]

In 1925, the Cole-Rice Law established a foundation formula which distributed state aid in a manner inversely related to local taxpaying ability. In also establishing a minimum flat grant, it guaranteed that all districts would receive some state aid, independent of their level of wealth. The preservation of a minimal share of total state aid for all districts was the element of the system that limited the equalizing thrust of the formula. Later developments were to make this factor even more important as all sorts of "save harmless" provisions were enacted that protected and preserved existing state aid shares of wealthier districts.

The exact determination of formula construction and operation was left to the legislature, and became in fact a major part of its business. Concern with the formula became a priority of legislators and they viewed it as an important indicator of their effectiveness in serving their districts. It was certain to be one issue that the voters back home would follow closely inasmuch as the amount of state educational aid had an immediate impact on funds which would have to be raised by local property taxes. Close attention was paid, therefore, to the educational aid process and the impact of the aid formula on local districts. This motivated legislators to be concerned primarily with protecting and preserving the shares of their school district constituencies.

The various changes that have occurred in the state aid formula reflect the intense conflicts generated over distribution of educational aid. Although it is beyond the scope of this work to discuss in detail all the changes that have been made, the historical development of the state aid formula has significant implications for our concern with the goal of equality. As we will demonstrate later in this chapter, all the various changes in the formula have neither significantly reduced the disparities in per pupil expenditures, nor weakened the positive relationship between expenditures and wealth. As a matter of fact, the differences have been increasing. (See Table 4 and Chart 2.)

The operating aid formula is essentially an aid ratio which is constructed to determine the amount of state funds to be distributed to each school district. It is philosophically and conceptually the embodiment of the original foundation aid formula conceived of by Strayer, Haig and Cubberly as the means by which to ensure that minimum levels of funding adequacy are guaranteed by the state for each child.

The operating aid formula has had a long and complicated history as different groups and interests seek to change and manipulate the formula to advance their interests. The elaboration of details regarding its historical development would require a volume by itself. Our main interest is in demonstrating why the so-called state equalizing formula has not eliminated inequalities, and in fact per-pupil expenditure differences have actually widened at the same time that equity goals are proclaimed as the justification for changing the formula. For purposes of clarity and substantiation of the discussion in this and succeeding chapters, we shall delineate some major features of the current state aid formula, leaving aside the mathematical and computational aspects of calculation.[14] (Table 5 in the Statistical Appendix outlines the current New York State operating formula.)

The legislature annually determines a ceiling level in which the state will share educational expenditures with localities. Also to be determined by the legislature are the various refinements and adaptations in the design and methodology of the formula that are regularly developed as part of the process of coalition building and budget passage. The basic operating aid formula determines distribution of the major portion of state aid, which amounted to $4.9 billion out of $8.9 billion, representing 55.1 percent of total state aid for the 1990-91 school year.[15]

The distribution of aid is determined by the wealth of a school district relative to average statewide wealth. Historically, wealth was always measured as the property valuation per pupil. There was much criticism of the sole use of property as a measure of school district wealth, and in 1980 the legislature included a personal income factor as a determinant of wealth. At first, the effect of income was small since it was applied to only one tier of operating aid and involved only a small portion of the total aid. The legislature subsequently increased the power of income to affect the aid formula, and in 1984 it finally combined the two tiers and gave income a weight equal to that of property wealth.

A summary of the various forms of aid financed through state public school appropriations is presented for school years 1989-90 and 1990-91 in Table 6. (See Statistical Appendix.) It is clear that different state aids have been developed in response to perceptions of changing educational need. Nevertheless, money affected by the basic operating formula is always the major part of total state aid, and consequently at the center of the annual budgetary conflict over allocation and distribution. However, other forms of aid, representing the remainder of the $8.9 billion for the school year 1990-91, also reflect different tradeoffs and compromises among various educational and political interests—i.e., large city and suburban, upstate and downstate, rural and urban.

In addition to other formula-driven so-called "computerized aids" and the other various programs and categorical aids that are described in Table 6, a number of new programs merit special attention because of their strategic role in affecting the outcomes of the budget process. These aids often have an effect far greater than might be indicated by their relatively small size, and are consequently an important part of the subsequent discussion in Chapters 3 and 5.

Member item programs, discussed in greater detail in Chapter 3, are small sums set aside and earmarked for local community projects that are identified specifically with individual legislators and their areas. Because of the high degree of identification with the legislator and the local area, they have a political significance far greater than might be indicated by the sums involved. These grants are often used by the leadership in each house in order to appease the feelings of legislators who may be disaffected as a result of other budgetary outcomes. These special items totaled 12 million dollars in the 1990-91 school aid budget and involved projects in assembly and senate districts throughout the state.

If implementation of the state aid formula would result in a reduction of aid, and this is often the case with wealthier districts, the district can invoke a variety of save-harmless measures, in addition to a flat grant formula, that will ensure the maintenance of previous aid levels. Since save-harmless guarantees the maintenance of previous levels of state aid to all school districts, with the passage of each year the benefits flowing from save harmless are reduced as a result of the rising ceiling applied to the state aid formula.

Supplemental support and high tax aids, two new forms of aid recently developed, are forms of general aid designed to protect against the erosion of the value of save harmless. They drive more money to wealthier school districts that no longer benefit from the protections gained from a save-harmless status. Supplemental state aid and high tax aid compensate for some of these losses and are, therefore, an important part of recent budget negotiations, rising rapidly as a legislative response to the necessities of coalition building and the need to placate those, mostly wealthier, districts with more aid in order to gain their support for the state budget. For school year 1990-91, supplemental support aid totaled $429.4 million, a rise of 7.2 percent, and high tax aid $218 million, a rise of 14.1 percent.

Those who developed the aid formula sought to impose objective criteria in place of the political pressures that had previously determined the flow of state aid. They hoped at the same time to satisfy their philosophical values about a desirable role for the state to assume in compensating for local wealth differences. They appreciated the constraints of the political system and accepted the limits imposed by the system of local control and disparate property wealth resources. But they hoped that establishment of the foundation formula would remove aid from the political process of power and manipulation, and relate it instead to objective needs that could be measured, such as local wealth and student needs. They never expected the formula to achieve full equality, but neither did they foresee the extent to which their technical remedy, the aid formula, would in itself become a key issue in the annual political and budgetary process—subject to continual revisions and changes as groups mobilized to insure that the formula worked in their interests.

School District Boundaries and Local Wealth

The finance model that Strayer and Haig developed in 1925 proposed a sharing of school taxes between the state and the county. Knowing that statewide assumption of educational support would have been resisted by advocates of local control, they chose the county as the local source of support because it would at least lessen the range of inequalities. But this was rejected and the school district remained the local source of revenue. Due to the great inequalities in resources among districts, any attempt by the state to remedy these disparities would therefore be very costly.

The choice of the school district over the county undermined the ability of the formula to equalize, and thereby generated a system of educational finance, which to this day has defied attempts at reform. In fact, subsequent changes in the formula resulted in larger portions of state aid being devoted to non-equalizing purposes. Such changes included the basic flat grant provision, which assured each district a minimum sum per pupil, and save-harmless provisions which guaranteed districts as much aid, total or per pupil, in any given year as it had received the year before. The equalizing purposes of the formula were subverted so as to direct increasingly larger portions of state aid into districts with above-average wealth. The districts that benefited from this were then bound to resist any subsequently proposed changes that would reduce their shares, a fact that effectively destroyed the possibility of reform.

Various laws seeking to stimulate consolidation were passed, but had little effect. Chapter 675 of the Laws of 1925 provided, for the first time, a package of fiscal incentives to overcome local opposition to change. Incentives in the form of supplemental aid for operating, building and transportation needs were made available for periods up to fifteen years. The number of districts fell from some 10,000 in 1925 to 6,379 in 1940, 1,293 in 1960, 732 in 1980 and 718 in 1989.[16]

Aside from the long-term concern with interdistrict financial disparities, many other pressures built up to stimulate school district consolidation. The extension of universal free public education, and the increasing access to high school education, created a need for more specialized educational offerings than could be developed in a one-room schoolhouse. This resulted in the centralization of specialized educational services and in the consolidation of many small school districts so as to provide for increased services and economies of scale. While many local areas resisted these pressures—often for reasons of tradition, local control, or simply the preservation of special privilege— resistance usually melted before the inducements of significant state increases in aid for those districts which approved consolidation.

The Fleischmann Commission

In the 1970s, school district consolidation came to a virtual halt because of the lack of importance of the fiscal incentives for the remaining small districts. The privileges they have under the existing system are more valuable than the temporary fiscal benefits of consolidation. Consequently, it is very unlikely that there will be any more significant consolidation unless either the package of incentives is made more enticing or it is mandated by state law.

. The governance of education and school district organization is at the heart of the system of inequalities. Equalization attempts under the present "equalizing" state aid formula, without governmental reorganization, are therefore doomed to failure. This prompted the New York State Commission on the Quality, Cost and Financing of Elementary and Secondary Education, generally referred to as the Fleischmann Commission after the name of its chairman, to set forth in 1972 a reform proposal that confronted the issue of inequality and governance head on.

Realizing that the political and economic realities of education in New York State would never allow the enactment of a truly equalizing formula, the commission proposed fundamental and radical changes in the structure of school governance. It called for full state assumption of educational financing:

Taking account of the constitutional mandate, the equity consideration as described and other matters yet to be discussed, the Commission recommends that the State of New York undertake full funding
of educational costs. By full funding we mean that the state government become the governmental entity responsible for raising all or
practically all of the money to maintain and support public elementary and secondary schools except for that amount of money which
the Federal Government shall contribute.[17]

In addition to equalization, other benefits of full state financing
were also heralded, such as property tax relief, improvement of property tax administration, educational accountability and statewide standards regarding salary schedules. Full state support, it was argued, by
reducing local involvement with funding would also stimulate more effective community participation in substantive educational matters, an
issue which was a major concern at that time.

Opponents of the Fleischmann proposals stressed issues, such as
elimination of local control by the expansion of state government and
the mediocrity that would result from the lack of stimulation and in-
novation that now takes place in the more privileged "lighthouse"
school districts. Issues on lack of flexibility in educational decision
making and resource allocation were also stressed. Another significant
but usually neglected argument in support of the current system of
educational finance is that it serves at least one other major purpose—
the expansion of total monies allocated to education. A system of independent school districts stimulates maximum local contributions to
education, while also providing for large sums of state supplementa-
tion. To the extent that all funds come from the one source, the state, it
is likely that total funds spent on education would be less, especially if
education had to compete with other social needs and programs.

The reception granted the Fleischmann Commission proposal
presents an illuminating picture of education and politics in New York
State. The Commission's recommendations were totally ignored and
confined to shelves already crowded with the accumulated advice of
many past commissions and special studies; the more ambitious the
proposals, the more certain and rapid their demise.

Federal Aid

One important aspect has been missing from this discussion—the
role of federal aid. The equalizing impact of federal aid is minimal

because it has not grown as anticipated at the time that the Title I ESEA (Elementary and Secondary Education Act of 1965) program was created in 1965. The thrust of this program was to have resulted in significant equalization in favor of the children of the poor. It provided for a federal supplement to local school districts based upon the number of children from poverty backgrounds multiplied by one-half of the state's average per pupil expenditure.

Certainly this aid would have been of major import in reducing disparities and especially beneficial in alleviating the municipal overburden situation of the large central cities. The design of this aid program demonstrated the then greater responsiveness of the national administration to the needs of the poor. It also reflected the insulation of the federal government from the intense pressures felt in both local school districts and state capitals for more general forms of education aid. The fact of the matter is that the equalizing impact of Title I is now minimal both because appropriations did not grow as anticipated when the act was passed in 1965 and in fact declined significantly during the first term of the Reagan administration.[18]

Continual Formula Revisions

> The legislature has chosen to increase the number of non-operating aids, which produce disproportionate gains for higher spending districts.

> Many wealthy districts receive aid on a save-harmless basis. . . . As operating aid has been eroded and a greater proportion of state funds has been distributed in the form of grants or special formulas, higher spending districts have received aid increases over and above their save-harmless entitlements to operating aid.[19]

After more than a half-century of tinkering with the educational aid formula and after a decade of intense agitation for reform that eventually took the issue before the courts, a subject to be discussed in Chapter 4, disparities in expenditures per pupil have not been eliminated. They have in fact increased significantly. This is true regardless of the measure used and is reflected in Table 4 and Chart 2, in addition to the work of Joan Scheuer, who assessed the period between 1975 and 1982,[20] and the conclusions of Robert Berne and Leanna Stiefel,[21] who studied developments between 1965 and 1978. These findings are also confirmed in the work of the New York State Special Task Force on

Equity and Excellence in Education (the Rubin Task Force),[22] the most
recent governmental commission to study the subject.

The data are voluminous and the findings uniform. Comparisons
of interdistrict property wealth still exhibit great disparities, with
Scheuer's data revealing a ratio of 2.8 to 1 between the 10th and 90th
percentile in 1982. Ratios on expenditures showed a ratio of 9 to 1 between the highest and lowest spending district in 1982, and 1.8 to 1 between districts at the 90th and 10th percentile. She found that the range,
restricted range and coefficient of variation have increased between
1974 and 1982.[23] Chart 2 shows an expenditure gap of $3,913 per pupil
in 1986-87 between districts at the 10th and 90th percentile, a percent
difference of 106.7 percent. Concurring with the findings of Joan
Scheuer, Berne and Steinfel conclude that:

> For equal opportunity with respect to wealth in New York, one con-
> clusion is unaffected by the measure. In all fourteen years, there is a
> positive relationship between both objects and per pupil equalized
> property wealth. Thus equal opportunity with respect to wealth is ab-
> sent over the fourteen-year period. Overall, the trends in equal op-
> portunity with respect to wealth show a general worsening over the
> period, and again the latest part of the period, 1974 to 1978, displays
> the highest level of unequal opportunity with respect to wealth.[24]

The long-deplored characteristics of inequality remain stronger
than ever. The positive relationship between local property wealth and
educational expenditures shows a slight weakening, but the range of
disparities in expenditures has actually increased. Clearly, expenditures
are not allocated in relation to the educational needs of children, but are
dictated by differences in resources made available by local property
wealth. In fact, during the last few years, the situation has not improved
and indications are that it will worsen in the immediate future.

Failure of the Equalizing Formula

> Three factors limit the effectiveness of New York's operating aid for-
> mula in equalizing expenditures across the state's school districts.
> First, state aid supports only a minimum spending level. . . . As long
> as a significant portion of education spending is unequalized, educa-
> tion expenditures will vary directly with the wealth of the school dis-
> trict and the willingness of its residents to tax that wealth for schools.
> Second, a large number of school districts receive operating aid
> through flat grants and save harmless provisions since they are too

wealthy to qualify for equalization aid. The third factor that limits the equalizing impact of the formula is the size of the state share of educational expenditures. . . . Although the state contribution is estimated to be about $4.5 billion in 1982 to 1983, these dollars are insufficient to equalize expenditures in a state where wealth and expenditure disparities are large and spending levels are high.[25]

* * *

Professor Arvid Burke testified in the *Levittown* trial that "there has been no significant change since the 1925 enactment of the Cole law. The labels have changed and the exceptions and minor details have been changed, but the basic structure of 1925 has persisted to the present day."[26]

The reason the aid formula does not equalize significantly, even with the many revisions that have been enacted supposedly for that purpose, are clear once we examine some of the formula's components. First and foremost are the various protections built into the formula to insure that no wealthy district loses as a result of any revisions. This includes the basic flat grant per-pupil guarantee, the save-harmless total and the save-harmless, per-pupil guarantees. All three of these provisions are non-equalizing in the sense that they do not relate to fiscal relief or educational need, but solely maintain previous levels of aid. All districts are entitled to choose the precise manner in which they want their aid computed and, of course, they choose the variation that will result in the highest amount. Without these provisions, some districts would receive much less state aid. Consequently, the more that aid is allocated for such purposes, the less there will be available for equalization.

Special problems arise relating to differences in the governance of education in the Big Five cities (New York, Buffalo, Rochester, Yonkers and Syracuse) and the other school districts. The Big Five, which are all dependent school districts without their own taxing power, are included within and constrained by the constitutional tax and debt limits that apply to the parent municipality. At the same time, there is an increased necessity to divert municipal revenues to non-educational special big city needs, particularly the social service needs of poor people. This is what is referred to as municipal overburden—a situation that limits the ability of large cities to support education to the same degree as independent school districts with their own taxing powers but without the same big city problems or concentrations of poor people.

Although it is difficult to agree on a quantifiable measure of municipal overburden, there is general acknowledgement of its existence. The problem is how to incorporate this into the school aid formula with an operational measure that reflects the special needs of cities. The lack of attention to the unique condition of large cities has impaired the formula's responsiveness to their needs. This is because the equality-oriented features of the formula are directed to compensating for disparities in per-pupil property values among school districts, a matter that often does not relate to cities which may in fact have above-average property valuation. As long as the aid formula is oriented to wealth measures rather than to educational need measures, the special educational needs of large central cities will not be addressed.

Other elements of state aid explain why the equalizing formula fails. An often ignored issue is the relationship between operating aid, which is governed by the foundation formula, and other types of computerized aids, which are dispensed according to special formulae or allocated by lump sum for a specific purpose (categorical). These latter two are determined by different standards of eligibility and are not distributed with an equalizing intent. Therefore, the higher the amounts and proportion of state funds allocated for purposes other than operating aid, the less will be the equalizing impact of state aid. Table 6 lists the various types of aid and their cost for school years 1989-90 and 1990-91.

Another important reason state aid fails to equalize is that it only accounts for less than 50 percent of total school revenues. (See Table 2.) The percentage of revenues derived from state sources varies, with poorer districts generally more dependent on state aid than wealthier ones. This allows a great deal of latitude for local districts to increase revenues for education through raising more funds through local property taxes. Wealthier districts may do this even while implementing tax rates that are lower than those existing in many poorer districts. As long as there are no limits to local discretion, the power of the state to equalize expenditures is greatly limited, regardless of the impact of the state aid equalizing formula.

Too often, attention is paid only to the technical aspects of how the formula determines levels of state aid. This is the approach usually adopted by technicians, budgetary analysts and study commissions. There are many appeals to this "methodology." It involves mastery of technical and detailed knowledge. Since few have time to master the obscure minutiae of detail involved, those who do are in great demand by the political leadership. At the same time, it removes the subject from the realm of popular political discourse, leaving it as a matter to be resolved by legislative and political leaders together with technicians. This provides a camouflage, distracting attention from the manner in which political decisions affecting education aid are actually made.

The state aid formula absorbs the greatest interest of those who seek to affect change in the system. It acts as a lightning rod, attracting regular attention and scrutiny, generating myriads of proposals for adjustment and revision—often in the name of equity and equality. It has also taken on central importance in the annual dickering surrounding state budget adoption, a major chip to be used by contending sides as a part of tradeoffs in the budgetary contest. Regardless of which party controls the houses of the legislature or the executive branch, the results regarding equality tend to be the same. The costs of significant equalization, both in total money and redistribution impacts, are too great a burden for the political process to assume.

Proposals for reform and equalization regularly become discarded under pressure of demands for accommodation and budget adoption. And so after the rhetoric has spewed forth and passions have been spent, the issue of equality is once more dispensed with, although certain to be resurrected with ardor at the next budgetary cycle. Far more durable than the fleeting involvement of different political figures is the perennial recurring issue of equity in school finance.

It is impossible to understand the intent, practice and effects of state aid unless attention is given to the political and legislative process in New York State, and the manner in which the claimants—school districts, parents, children, educational interest groups, taxpayer groups, teacher unions—bring pressure to bear on legislators. The technical analysis is where cost studies and commissions stop. Since most studies and task forces are commissioned by state funds, there is an unspoken premise. Analysis and detail regarding technical matters are eagerly sought, for that area belongs to the neutral scientific domain of research. But consideration of the real determinants as to how decisions are made that affect the distribution of shares among affluent and poor districts—thereby determining equality of educational opportunity—this is the stuff of politics. It involves people, power, pressure and interests. Therefore, the real decision-making process is to be avoided—not spoken about publicly and certainly not be to discussed in writing by consultants and technicians. Discussion of this overlooked subject, which is central to understanding educational inequalities in New York State, follows in the next chapter.

NOTES

1. DeWitt Clinton, message to the state legislature, 1826.
2. Article XI, Section 1 of The Constitution of the State of New York. (Formerly No.1 of Article 9. Renumbered by the Constitutional Convention of 1938 and approved by vote of the people, November 8, 1938.)
3. For a discussion of these and other related developments, see David M. Ment, "Equality Concerns Reflected in the Establishment and Development of New York State's Public Education System," submitted as Appendix D to City-Plaintiffs' Court of Appeals brief in *Levittown v. Nyquist*, April 16, 1982. Also, "A Guide to Aid for Education in New York State," Joint Legislative Task Force on Education, New York State Legislature, Albany, N.Y., August 1978; and Arvid Burke, "Development of Public School Finance in New York State," Occasional Paper 14, New York State Finance Law Study, Vol. 5, Albany, N.Y., September 1978.
4. *Laws of New York, 1795* (Albany: State of New York, 1795), Chapter 75.
5. For a discussion of historical developments in school district organization, see, "School District Reorganization: An Introduction," The State Education Department, Albany, N.Y., December 1984, pp. 2-6. Also, "Better Education Through School District Reorganization," State Education Department, undated pamphlet; and "A Guide to School District Reorganization for New York State," State Education Department, Albany, N.Y., 1958.
6. Ment, op. cit., p. 41.
7. Section 1, Article IX (now Section 1, Article XI) of the New York State Constitution, effective January 1, 1895.
8. Burke, op. cit., p. 39.
9. Joan Scheuer, *State Aid for City Schools: Handbook for Policy Makers* (New York: New York City Board of Education, January 1985), p. 4.
10. Ellwood P. Cubberly, *School Funds and Their Apportionment* (New York: Teachers College, Columbia University, 1905), p. 17.
11. George D. Strayer, and Robert M. Haig, *The Financing of Education in the State of New York* (New York: Macmillan, 1923).
12. Ibid.
13. Henry C. Morrison, *School Revenue* (Chicago: University of Chicago Press, 1930), p. 194.

14. For an elaborate and detailed discussion and explanation of different parts of the formula, see Joel S. Berke, Margaret E. Goertz and Richard J. Coley, *Politicians, Judges and City Schools; Reforming School Finance in New York* (New York: Russel Sage Foundation, 1984), passim.

15. "Description of 1990-91 New York State School Aid Programs," Education Unit, New York State Division of the Budget; Albany, N.Y., November 15, 1990, Table II-A.

16. *Annual Educational Summary, 1988-1989* (Albany: Information Center on Education, State Education Department, 1990), Table 2, p. 4.

17. *Report of the New York State Commission on the Quality, Cost and Financing of Elementary and Secondary Education, 1972*, Vol. 1 (Albany: The Commission, 1972), p. 62.

18. D. Lee Bawden and John L. Palmer, "Social Policy: Changing the Welfare State," *The Reagan Record*, John L. Palmer and Isabel V. Sawhill, eds. (Washington, DC: The Urban Institute, 1984), p. 185.

19. Scheuer, op. cit., p. 35.

20. Joan Scheuer, "The Equity of New York State's System of Financing Schools: An Update," *Journal of Education Finance* 9, No. 1 (Summer 1983), pp. 79-87.

21. Robert Berne and Leanna Stiefel, *The Measurement of Equity in School Finance: Conceptual, Methodological and Empirical Dimensions* (Baltimore: The Johns Hopkins University Press, 1984).

22. *Report and Recommendations of the New York State Special Task Force on Equity and Excellence in Education*, Albany, N.Y., Feburary 1982.

23. Scheuer, "Equity," op. cit., p. 83.

24. Berne and Stiefel, op. cit., p. 286.

25. Berke, et. al., op. cit., pp. 132-133.

26. See trial transcript of *Levittown v. Nyquist*, 94 Misc. 2d 466, p. A3951.

3.
POLITICS AND POWER IN NEW YORK STATE

Regardless of the simpleness and equity of school finance legislation when it is first passed, it soon is amended by provisions designed to foster the interests of particular groups. These special provisions are frequently disequalizing, and at the least complicate the finance system so much that scarcely anyone (including state officials who administer it) completely understands it. As an example, various 'save harmless' provisions were added to the New York law over time. These were intended to keep districts from receiving less money under a new law than under a previous law. The result was that there were 36 different ways to calculate a district's state aid, and each district was entitled to use whichever calculation brought the most money.

> —Walter Garms, James Guthrie and
> Lawrence Pierce, *School Finance*

* * *

Those who love the law, like those who love sausage, should never be present when it is being made.

> —Chancellor Otto Von Bismarck

In Chapter 2, we analyzed the history of educational inequality in New York State and focused upon the relationships between disparities in per-pupil property values, the fragmented independent school district form of educational governance and the mystique of an allegedly

44

equalizing state aid formula which fails to equalize. The emphasis on inequality has absorbed the attention of educational reformers for the better part of a century until this very day. Hence, the proliferation of studies, commissions and special task forces which put forth proposals designed to change governance and taxing arrangements or affect compensating mechanisms in the aid formula.

A fundamental fallacy has undermined the efforts of reformers. They usually assume that the problem essentially is due to defects in the structure of administration and governance, and therefore remediable through the development of well-crafted proposals for reorganization and redesign. This leads to a faith that commissions and special task forces will research the matter, determine what is good and then submit proposals for implementation. The one subject that is left out of the discussion and analysis—a taboo not to be broken—is the question of politics and power and how the political system works to preserve and maintain the interests of the privileged against the claims of the disadvantaged who seek to improve their situation.

Of course, those involved in the process have an important reason for proceeding in this manner. The legislative leadership, the rank and file legislators and the staff technicians must work together in order to forge a compromise that will facilitate adoption of the annual budget. In order to function effectively, it is necessary to conceal manipulations of the legislative process from public awareness. Thus, much of the wheeling and dealing that goes into the development of the educational aid package is never brought to public attention.

A similar set of constraints affects the behavior of outsiders who study the system and are engaged in recommending change and reform. They are often appointed and funded by the political leadership in the executive and legislative branches, for whose consideration reports and recommendations must be submitted. It follows, therefore, that recognition, approval and standing are highly dependent upon conforming to the etiquette and boundaries of political discourse. This is also evident in the case of the experts and technicians employed by the state government or the legislature. It is less clearly evident, but nonetheless true regarding influential outsiders—those academics and consultants brought into the process to contribute expertise and provide a hallowing aura of disinterested, scientific, professional competence.

All participants must behave in conformance with the canons of professional research and consultancy. However, attention to politics and power, the real driving forces of the system, and the constraints limiting attempts at change are matters to be handled gingerly. Certainly mention is made regularly of the so-called political realities of the situation and politics is almost always at the center of awareness. But the rule is always followed: think and talk but never write and inform, and certainly keep such matters out of proposals or public discussions. In this manner, the traditional separation and dichotomy between politics and education is maintained as studies, commissions and proposals proliferate, leaving a repository of passionate and sincere but unheeded calls for change, viewed with bemused toleration and skepticism by veteran observers who have seen the game played on many an occasion.

In this chapter, we shall address the manner in which the political process functions so as to assure that educational equality—in the sense of equal expenditures per pupil—cannot be attained.

The Political System

The political system of New York State[1] is characterized by two strong parties, which are highly competitive, and a strong chief executive who often may not command the loyalty of his party. The two houses may shift in party domination, although it is presently the case that the Democrats have controlled the New York State Assembly since the elections of 1974 and Republicans have controlled the New York State Senate since 1939, with the exception of 1965.

There are one hundred fifty members in the assembly and sixty-one in the senate. Since the impact of *Baker v. Carr* in 1962, both houses have been apportioned on a one-man, one-vote basis, resulting today in a population variation of only plus or minus 4.8 percent in the assembly and plus or minus 2.7 percent in the senate. Conventional wisdom anticipated that reapportionment would result in a shift of legislative political dominance from rural areas to cities. However, long-developing demographic trends culminated in a shift of population from the cities to the suburbs sufficient to cause a reduction in the cities' share of the state's population. And although the shift was insufficient to give the suburbs a majority of the state population, there was enough growth to make suburban legislators the dominant force in the emerging suburban-rural coalition to which political power shifted after *Baker v. Carr*.

The Contestants

> ... there has to be some outside force brought into this other than the Legislature because to get any rational pattern today in these laws is almost impossible because there is only one criterion that these more powerful school districts apply to any law, and that is, "How much do I get out of it? Do I get more money than I got before?" And "it doesn't make any difference whether they got too much before; they want more than they got before."[2]

Democratic seats are more heavily concentrated in the cities, of which the five largest have dependent school districts, where there is neither a separate education budget approval process nor school taxing power. Republican members tend to come from legislative districts that represent independent school districts where such powers do exist. However, since one legislative district may comprise as many as seventy-two school districts, its school district composition will often encompass both property-wealthy and property-poor districts. All school districts have an important interest in the content of state legislation affecting aid formulas, curriculum mandates and other cost-related school matters. For some, increases in state aid facilitate lowering the burden of local property taxes. Other districts may use increased state aid to avoid increasing local taxes as costs rise, and still others may use increased state aid in conjunction with higher local taxes to provide for an enriched quality of education.

The intensity of involvement with the process may vary, especially regarding different styles of behavior encountered among independent and dependent school districts.

All school districts, except the "Big Five"—those city school districts with more than 125,000 population—are independent. Since these large cities do not have a separate budget approval and property tax structure for education, this results in important distinctions in the manner in which issues of school finance are dealt with, a matter which we shall point to later in our analysis.

Districts vary in size, from Rhinecliff with 122 students to New York City with 925,246 students.[3] With the exception of New York City, no school district can afford full-time representation in the state capital. Consequently, there is great reliance on a variety of citizen, professional and political lobbying groups to present the case for school aid. While there are factors making for divisiveness and conflict among districts regarding wealth, educational needs and attitudes toward education, there is agreement regarding the need for political pressure to stimulate the state to spend more money for education.

To the extent that more state aid for education affects all other aspects of the budget, conflicts over educational spending will involve various other political and economic interests which are not directly involved with education. Businessmen concerned with taxes, labor groups worried about the needs of their workers, lobbyists for a variety of diverse interests, civil service groups representing noneducational employees—all these often press for levels of state funding that conflict with special demands for more educational funds.

The Budgetary Process

In order to understand the manner in which choices are made regarding the distribution of monies for education, we must focus on the annual cycle of proposals, counter-proposals and compromises involved in the decision-making process. It is around this process that the various groups converge to protect their interests and impose their will. With the question of resource distribution, we can observe the shaping of disparate interests into coalitions and the merging of separate issue majorities into the grand majority necessary to gain the approval of the majority conference in both houses of the legislature.

Although the process may vary significantly from year to year, depending upon the prevailing political and economic winds and the differing personalities involved, there is a certain consistency imposed by the necessity to meet budgetary deadlines. In the end, budgets must be passed in conformance with schedules and deadlines. And for that reason, what may strike the uninformed observer as a disorganized jumble of intense uncoordinated activity is in reality all part of a patterned movement toward a clear and coherent purpose, the enactment of legislation and the disbursement of money. Initial differences are often so great as to resist any notion of reconciliation and it is more than likely that, without the intervention of consensus-forming mechanisms and time constraints, decisions could never be reached. To understand how these gaps are bridged, we turn our attention to the unfolding of the events themselves. But before we do this, a few words about changing institutional relationships and their impact on the decision-making process.

Changing Political Patterns

The arrangements which we are going to describe represent a relatively new configuration of relationships affecting the annual distribution of state educational aid to localities. Before 1976, decisions regarding state aid to education were made by the governor and the legislative leadership *after* submission by the governor of his executive budget. The executive budget merely contained an appropriate lump sum amount for education without specification of the formula that would determine distribution of the aid. It was only under Governor Carey in his 1976-77 budget submission that the executive budget first included specific recommendations for state aid to schools. This change stemmed from Governor Carey's style of aggressive competition and conflict with the legislature for control of the budgetary process. However, at just about the time the governor began to include his education formula recommendations in the executive budget, other events transpired that diluted the importance of the formula as the ultimate real world determinant of state education aid.

The first of these other events began in the early 1970s, with the desire on the part of Governors Rockefeller and Wilson to increase New York City's share of school aid. Their motives were based on an appreciation of the educational needs of New York City children and their perception of the equities involved. Lieutenant Governor Wilson's commitment was reinforced by the political need to dilute his conservative image and assume the somewhat more liberal political coloration needed to run successfully in the upcoming statewide gubernatorial election. Increasing the city's share was made more difficult at that time because property wealth per pupil was increasing faster in the city than in the rest of the state, a fact that would normally cause the aid formula to drive more money away from, rather than to, the city.

A number of devices were then devised by Governor Rockefeller and his staff to avert this possibility and channel more aid to the city. In 1968-69, New York City operating aid was for the first time computed on a borough basis rather than citywide. Consequently, the potential decreases in total school aid to New York City attributable to rising property values in Manhattan were more than compensated for by utilizing five different property valuations.

Another formula change initiated in 1974 was also intended to increase educational aid to New York City. The 1974 legislature adopted special services aid for the Big Five cities and also began to change the system of pupil counts in order to make the formula outcomes more favorable to cities. It was also at that time that the pupil count was first weighted for students with special educational needs and physical handicaps. Additional pupil count changes along a similar vein were introduced during the following years.

At the same time that the above changes were taking place, the State Board of Equalization and Assessment changed the timetable for the introduction of the market value survey used to determine relative district per-pupil wealth. The introduction of these new property wealth relationships, coinciding with the New York City fiscal crisis, demonstrated in an unexpected manner the deterioration of New York City property valuations relative to the rest of the state. Also, at that time, New York City was experiencing a relatively smaller decline in number of pupils than the rest of the state.

These exogenous factors, by revealing New York City as relatively poorer in terms of per-pupil property wealth, combined with the previously discussed intentional formula changes, would have resulted in greatly increasing the city's share of formula determined state aid. The impact would have resulted in an undermining of the traditionally acceptable division between New York City and the rest of the state, and would have weakened Republican control outside New York City.

In addition, during the same period, significant changes occurred in the political system of New York State. The Democrats assumed control of both the executive branch and the assembly in 1975, while the Republicans retained control of the senate. This new reality of two-party involvement required the introduction of mechanisms to allow negotiated bipartisan compromises in place of the prior arrangements that reflected deals between a Republican governor and leaders of both houses who came from his own party.

The current system of educational policy decision making reflects a brokered system of compromise and conflict resolution among the majority leadership of both houses. Although the Democrats in the majority of the assembly are strongly tied to city interests, they have, for purposes of obtaining and retaining majority control, been forced to moderate their claims for more education aid for the city. This has resulted in a negotiated compromise that prevents the formula from accomplishing the equalizing results that would have occurred if its impact were not impeded by a prior compromise regarding distribution of shares between New York City and the rest of the state.

The effects of this manner of decision making are most clearly evidenced in the fiscal outcomes of the last few years. During this period, state education aid increased at a rate higher than during most of the preceding years, in excess of 10 percent for all the years but one during the period between 1978 and 1989. (See Table 7.) It is only during the succeeding fiscal crisis that we begin to see a reversal of this trend.

A major factor in the growth that occurred was because the assembly majority under Speaker Fink committed itself to education as a major priority. However, in spite of these large increases, progress toward equalization of fiscal disparities did not occur. In fact, the spread between the 10th and 90th decile of school districts increased from a difference of 92.5 percent to 106.7 percent during this period of great growth in state aid. (See Table 4 and Chart 2.)

This reflects the fact that even large increases in state aid do not lessen fiscal disparities because political tradeoffs necessary for a budgetary resolution dictate that additional monies must also be made available for all the other school districts. This tendency is especially reinforced by recent developments which have shifted the major goals of educational reform away from equity and equality to an emphasis on "excellence in education."

We believe it possible that this form of politically brokered compromise is likely to be the dominant form of decision making in those states with divided control of the two houses of the legislature. We shall now consider the specific mechanics of how this system works in New York State and how it manages to achieve agreements within the cycle of the annual budgetary process.

The Leaders Come Together

The first act begins with the determination of the parameters regarding expected revenues and expenditures. The first stage in the process is setting the framework in the initial executive budget submisssion. Some years are "better" than others. "Better" means more money available to satisfy the most interests and reduce the number of hard choices that must be made among competing claimants.

All are aware that the governor's budget proposals will be far from the actual outcomes, especially in state education aid which is a key province of legislative initiative. This is demonstrated most clearly in recent executive budget proposals which have called for elimination or significant reduction in save-harmless clauses, the so-called "Robin Hood" proposals. These proposals are regularly given short shrift by the legislature, a large number of the membership finding their content antagonistic to their personal goals and needs for re-election.

Nevertheless, the governor's initial budget submission, which kicks off the opening of each legislative session, is most important in setting the parameters and framework of the total budget and the relationships of the different parts. Regardless of the various outcomes, it impresses upon all the participants some notion of limits and discipline regarding possibilities and tradeoffs that will engage their attention and energies during the rest of the legislative session.

The first tentative "coming together of the minds" occurs at a meeting between the speaker of the assembly and the temporary president of the senate or of their chief fiscal lieutenants, where the basic parameters of the budget are agreed upon, i.e., total revenue projections and expenditures based both on their own separate estimates and the proposals of the governor in the executive budget presented to the legislature. All have in mind not only the economic aspects of the budget, but also the electoral prospects most immediately ahead.

The electoral picture in conjunction with economic conditions affects the answer to the perennial dilemma: Will it be spending time, tax cut time or a year to stand pat? Once the two leaders are agreed on the aggregate dimensions of the budget, the next major issue to be dealt with is the specific allocation for increases in state aid to education. This in turn is dependent not only on the agreed-upon general parameters of the budget, but also on the mood of the public in relation to education, the commitments to increase aid made by the leaders during the past year and adherence to the "rules of the game" discussed in the latter part of this chapter.

Determining the New York City Share

Albany's traditional upstate-downstate battle over New York State's education budget usually leaves New York City slighted on state aid. This year the maneuvering threatens to deepen the insult.

State school aid is supposedly distributed on the basis of complicated formlas that take into account each district's relative wealth and special needs. In practice, the legislators first determine the city's share of state aid, and then adjust the formulas to fit. Upstaters wield the upper hand, permitting the city only 31.5% of the state's education funds, though it has 35% of student enrollment—a current shortfall of $334 million.[4]

The key factor of the amount of education aid for New York City is the next thing to be determined. The two leaders actually determine the proportion of the agreed increase in aid that will be allocated to New York City. It is necessary to agree on the New York City share before the legislature's technicians are in a position to allocate the agreed-upon increase to the various elements of the formula. This stage in the process has been unnoticed and its importance overlooked because observers have usually concerned themselves with outcomes and not with the actual mechanics of decision making.

The conventional wisdom is that the state aid to education formula determines the allocation of state aid for New York City and the rest of the state, and that it is therefore the formula which is responsible for existing inequities and disparities. Actually, the aid formula has absolutely no effect on equity vis-à-vis New York City and the rest of the state. It is the specific decision made by the leaders regarding the New York City proportion of the total statewide share that determines equity for the city.

The actual share of total state education aid to New York City has risen significantly over the last two decades, at the same time that absolute levels of state aid have also increased greatly. Table 8 in the Statistical Appendix demonstrates the increases in the New York City share, which occurred during the period between 1965-66 and 1984-85. Later, more detailed work by Jerry Miner indicated that the rate of increase in the city share of state aid has declined with the city share of state aid holding steady at about 33 percent, rising from 33.0 to 33.6 from 1987 to 1990.[5] With the level of state aid at almost $9 billion during the 1990-91 school year, each percentage point change could result in an additional amount of $90 million. Since the total amount of aid is limited, additions for the city must come at the expense of other districts, thereby increasing the intensity of competition.

The division agreed upon by the leaders is transmitted by their two fiscal secretaries to their respective staffs. The legislative staff technicians then fine-tune the formula so that the mathematical outcome of the application of the formula results in both the disbursement of the agreed aggregate sum and also in the allocation of the agreed shares between New York City and the rest of the state. The agreed proportional distribution actually drives and determines the elements of the formula.

All legislative insiders agree that there is absolutely no factual question, but that these decisions are made by the leaders prior to the adjusting of the formula by the technicians. The fine-tuning of the formula is simply the means to assure the achievement of the pre-ordained percentages. It is because the fine-tuning process is unrelated to the objectives of the formula that the resulting statutory formulation appears to be schizophrenic; the various elements work at counter purposes and effectively cancel themselves out. Essentially, the formula serves no function and has no substantive impact with respect to New York City. It merely serves as a camouflaging device to mask and obscure the real decision-making process.

After being informed of the gross amount of education aid and New York City's share, the technicians then proceed to determine the distribution of the total share going to the rest of the state. Attention is directed to questions of allocation among different areas of the state and its diverse population groups. Decisions must be reached about the formulae or arrangements that will lay the basis for accords among the various competing constituencies. The staff must regularly report back to the leadership and keep them informed about important decisions that are being made, and must get approval and consent to any adjustments being made in the distribution.

There are seven hundred and twenty operating independent school districts receiving state aid, plus the five dependent city school districts of over 125,000 population. All districts seek, at the very minimum, to retain their previous shares, as measured by either per-pupil expenditures or the sum total of state aid. Of course, all districts desire additional aid in whatever form it may be given, general, categorical or special member programs. The outside parameters of the fiscal range of possibilities flows from the original decisions of the leaders. The actual outcomes emerge from negotiations between interest groups, members of the education committees, professional staff technicians and the rank-and-file legislators.

Distributing the Money

It is the task of the leadership to develop the framework for an agreement. It remains for staff and committee members to work out the details of distribution—which districts are to receive what shares of the pie. This process reflects the different strategies and techniques that are used to forge coalitions and move toward consensus. This process also must be viewed with two tiered discernment, for it takes place separately in the assembly and the senate, and its distinctiveness is enhanced by the fact that the houses are usually responsive to different party majorities. In fact, an important factor in determining the final outcome will usually be which house chooses to take the initiative in proposing terms for an agreement.

The assembly must be more responsive to the needs of the cities, which are responsible for the major part of the Democratic majority. At the same time, the additional votes necessary for a majority are usually secured from suburban areas. Consequently, a delicate balance must be maintained in forging the majority vote in the assembly. Responsiveness is required to the demands of New York City for an equal and hopefully greater proportion of the increase in new monies. Great solicitude and special care must also be shown to those Democratic legislators who won suburban districts by a narrow majority, and are, therefore, more vulnerable to Republican charges of voting for New York City interests at the expense of their own district. These suburban Democrats must be given special attention since they provide the margin of the assembly's Democratic majority.

On the other hand, the senate, Republican for all but one of the last forty-six years, represents a different bonding of interests on matters related to school aid. Its Republican majority is composed primarily of upstate urban and rural and downstate suburban members, and a handful of New York City members representing conservative districts within the city. Senators represent districts of a far greater population size than do members of the assembly, about two-and-a-half times as large. They are, consequently, likely to have a greater variety of differing constituency needs. However, most members of the Republican senate majority represent school districts of wealth, ethnic and municipal overburden characteristics, differing from New York City, the interests of which are represented by Democratic members of the assembly.

Such is the craft and ingenuity that recur annually as the great school aid struggle is launched. The struggle reflects conflicts between upstate and downstate, the city versus the suburbs and Republicans against Democrats. The eventual compromise and cooperation occur between senate and assembly majority conferences, each wedded to interests reflecting different elements of the struggle. Hence, the key role is played by staff as they master and manipulate substance and form, aggregate bottom lines and special add-ons. With calculating appraisals, they simultaneously assess progress toward two goals—the support of each majority conference and reconciliation of the differences between the two houses. Such are the determinants of assertion and compromise as the game is played out to its denouement.

Two additional factors must be included in our analysis of the struggle over state aid to education: governmental structure and the differing composition of each majority's base of support. Usually more than half of the Democratic assembly members come from New York City, which is a single school district where there is no direct voter participation in the approval of school budgets and no special property tax for education. Therefore, the degree of intensity and concern with school support that exists in the independent school districts is likely to be greater than that encountered in the city.

There is also the fact that New York City members must concern themselves with a variety of non-educational state support programs for such purposes as public assistance, medicaid, public health and public housing which usually provide less benefits to the higher income areas outside New York City. City legislators are more likely to focus with intensity on those concerns that they perceive to be of greater importance to their constituents. On the other hand, many legislators representing independent school districts focus on state aid to education, which to a greater or lesser extent must be directly supplemented by local real property taxes.

At the same time, there is somewhat of a reverse twist at work. Both majorities—to a greater extent in the assembly, less in the senate—are dependent on New York City votes. Both parties are also dependent upon the votes of suburban legislators. Consequently, with respect to state aid to education there is an interlocking of interests that cuts across both house and party lines and facilitates the development of an agreement among both parties and houses.

These factors combine to make education an extremely political, but a generally less partisan issue than others. Party labels alone do not sufficiently denote the clash of interests or goals pursued. The staff specialists are well aware of this fact as they fine-tune their proposals within the leadership-ordained parameters, with one eye on their own majority conference and the other on the process under way in the majority party conference of the other house. The final product must reflect, to a greater or lesser degree, the educational, fiscal and political needs of the members.

Therefore, the technicians must pay attention to the impact of the formula upon the city as a constraint to the development of a majority in each of the party conferences and in the subsequent final legislative compromise. They must also pay attention to the impact of the formula on suburban school interests. Both suburban and city school interests are thus looked after by significant parts of the party majority in each house, assuring the basis of a working consensus in the positions that are ultimately developed.

As each conference moves toward development of the final education aid package, an important element is yet to be resolved. That is the question of who goes first. The leadership and staff persons in each house are concerned that their proposals be within an acceptable range of accommodation with that of the other house. But an important part of the process relates to which group will take the initiative and how the initial parameters are staked out. Earlier, the overall aggregates regarding the total sum were agreed upon by the leadership; now, the distribution of specific dollars must be reconciled with the totals. And this distribution includes not only the general operating aid included in the state aid formula, but also allotments for the various categorical programs as well as special member items often referred to as "bullet aids."

The refinement of the general aid formula, the allocation for special categorical programs, the tailoring of programs aimed specifically for individual legislators and their school districts—these are the subjects of bargaining that secure a conference resolution in each house and provide the basis for eventual compromise and resolution between the two houses. The nature of education politics in New York makes it highly unlikely that the governor will attempt to affect significant change after the reaching of an agreement between the two houses. But before the stage of gubernatorial action can be reached, all sides in the legislature, including the leadership, must conform to the rules of the game. And it is these rules that determine the structure, the process (and therefore the outcomes) and also set limits to the equalizing effects that might ensue. Understanding these rules and how they work is a necessary prerequisite for gauging the likely results as well as understanding why it is that a significant lessening of disparities cannot be achieved.

The Rules of the Game

Governor Carey wants to redirect a few hundred million from rich to poor districts by such devices as cutting out minimum grants and "save-harmless" provisions—steps widely regarded as politically impossible in view of the political strength of the wealthy districts. As Mr. Kelly [a Ford Foundation official] observed: "There's a tradition of legislative courtesy that you don't finance your dinner out of someone else's lunch.[6]

* * *

Why then, it may be asked, have so few of our proposals been accepted and translated into law in the intervening three years? Politi-

cally, the basic problem (referred to again in the proposed draft) is
what we used to call, "Who wins; who loses?" As you will recall, in
the Fleischmann Report we made a detailed study of this matter,
covering every principal municipality in the State. I do not recall that
any legislator from a district that would have suffered from our
proposal came forth to endorse it.[7]

The fundamental outcome, which all are commited to, is that there
will be no losers. All school districts must receive as much as they did
the previous year. This is the minimum outcome that each legislator
must be able to achieve for his school districts. Failure to do so would
undermine his prospects for re-election, for it would subject him to charges of double failure—a decline in state aid and the resulting necessity
to increase local property taxes to compensate for the loss in state school
money. To avoid this political calamity, various save-harmless
provisions are appended to the equalizing formula, but this reduces even
more the amount of money available for equalization purposes.

The needs and wishes of the individual legislators of the majority
party in each house of the legislature are given paramount consideration. A key to the process is the enforcement of strict party discipline in
the actual voting on the budget, a fact which requires that members be
involved and consulted whenever the interests of their constituencies
are directly affected so as to assure no adverse political consequences.
Since final passage of the education budget will require approval of the
majority conference in each house, the approval of members is always
of highest concern. The majority cannot afford to lose support among
its members, lest its dominance be threatened. Also, since the majority
in each house is anxious to maintain its control in future elections, special attention is given to the needs of members who were elected by
very slim majorities in order to enhance their re-election prospects.

However, regarding members' needs and interests for state aid for
education, discernment is required. Assembly districts contain an
average population of 117,000 and the senate, 288,000. But school districts range in population from very small ones to New York City's
925,000 students. Consequently, we can expect to see a great variety in
the characteristics of school districts that each legislator represents.
However, not every school district is of equal importance to a legislator.
The numerical basis of political strength may be tied to a population attached to a few particular districts and this dictates the legislator's special attention to these districts.

The function of staff is crucial in these circumstances. Staff
specialists and technicians attached to committees, such as Education,

Assembly Ways and Means or Senate Finance, must be aware of the constraints affecting the welding of a majority. They must pay attention to each member's needs and interests, but must also give special attention to marginal districts and special issues that are regarded as essential. Consequently, special member items, or "bullet grants," are included in budgets. Attentiveness and responsiveness on the part of staff to special needs of members is necessary for a conference majority. Since every legislator's prime concern is political survival, the staff must be concerned with the effects of their proposals on each member's chances for re-election.

For example, the commitment to equality on the part of Democrats from cities and other less affluent areas will be lessened by the need to appease the interests of Democratic members from the more privileged suburban districts, who reflect the interests of their constituencies for more aid and less equalization. The leadership and most members will therefore refrain from bringing pressure on marginal members to conform to the interests of the majority, lest this result in forcing positions that will undermine their seats and the preservation of Democratic majority rule. This accounts for the fact, explained earlier, that it is possible to have large absolute increases in total state aid without having any impact on interdistrict disparities.

Similarly, in the senate, the interests of the majority representing more affluent areas must be reconciled with the need to protect Republican members from the city and poor rural areas where constituencies stand to benefit from progress toward equalization. Thus, the Democratic and Republican conferences in the assembly and the senate respectively tend to converge in goals and tactics, in a manner more than might be expected solely through assessment of the needs of most of their members. This has the effect of lessening the intensity of commitment to equality and the reduction of disparities, leading instead to tradeoffs within and between the parties involving other goals.

As noted earlier, not all school districts are equally important to a legislator. They will be of differing size and often also reflect interests based upon differing wealth, income and educational expenditure levels as well as contrasting student characteristics and educational needs.[8] (See Table 9.) An additional complication results from the fact that legislative and school districts are not contiguous. A school district may cross over a number of legislative boundaries, although this is more likely to be the case in assembly districts than in the larger senate districts. Consequently, a legislator often represents many whole school districts, and also parts of districts that he shares with other legislators.

The question for the legislator is which school districts are of crucial importance as a political and electoral base of support. The longer the tenure, the more clear this becomes, and the more the legislator focuses efforts on protecting those particular districts. To determine which are most important and to make sure that they are taken care of, the legislator maintains close contact with educational staff persons to keep apprised of outcomes resulting from different aid proposals and how they are likely to affect each school district. Therefore, some school districts become more important than others in a manner not related to issues of equity or educational need, but rather to the political interests of the legislator.

Education is an issue of great importance in the state political system, involving the largest amounts of state aid, and usually the greatest attention and dispute. Education, however, is not equally important to all members. Just as all school districts are not equally important to a member, so too all members are not equally interested in education. Certainly all members seek more aid for their constituents, but the results are not as important to some as to others.

For some members, especially those in inner-city areas of the Big Five cities, other non-educational state-supported services, such as public assistance, housing and medicaid, may be of greater importance. These members may also feel less interest and pressure from their constituents regarding education, since there is neither a separate school budget vote nor a local school property tax. Consequently, these members may exert their greatest efforts for more resources in non-educational areas, and may often view this goal as being of greater importance than more money for education.

Other members, especially those from affluent suburban areas with independent school districts, may believe that education is the single issue that will most be used to measure their effectiveness, especially since it directly affects local property taxes for education. Therefore, there are significant differences in the intensity of concern and energy brought to bear on issues of school finance, directly related to the type of constituency being represented.

A major determinant of the political and budgetary process in education, as in all other matters, is the existence of strong party discipline in both houses. This means that critical decisions and compromises are made within each house's majority conference. The nature of subsequent compromises between the conferences is determined by limits set by the leadership in consultation with their members. In both the assembly and the senate, the majority party rules and controls all matters.

The basic framework of legislative operations is predicated upon party discipline. Rewards for compliance are many, such as committee chairmanships, extra expense allowances, additional and special staff assignments, choice offices, preferential treatment of special program requests and special help, including financial assistance in re-election efforts. Sanctions for breaches of party discipline include censure and rebuke, the loss of choice committee and task force assignments, isolation from the good graces of the leadership and fellow members, as well as the loss of many other privileges cited above.

Party discipline is the essential element involved in the management of each house. The strong leader pays attention to potential disruption and moves to co-opt possible disaffection. It is because of strong party discipline that the machinery of each house works smoothly. It is fear over the loss of power and perquisites associated with majority control that motivates the allegiance of members. And it is the desire to assure the continuance of majority control that makes the leadership and members responsive to the needs and interests of all majority members, thereby decreasing reliance upon compulsion and coercion to achieve unanimity.

Regarding the issue of lessening fiscal inequalities among school districts, the dictates of coalition building and party discipline result in a shift in orientation among Democratic and Republican conferences. The need for each majority conference to be more sensitive to the electoral needs of its marginal members results in the Republican Senate Conference being more receptive to equalization proposals and the Assembly Democratic Conference being less aggressive than might have been expected, given the local pressures on most of their members. Intense ideological differences related to the struggle for educational equality are moderated by the necessity of coalescing for the sake of preserving legislative dominance.

State monies are spent for education in a variety of ways. Most of our attention has been focused on operating formula aid, which is the single greatest source of state aid, and which is directly tied to property wealth and income formula factors that cause it to have an equalizing tendency. Other forms of aid, in addition to general operating aid, include formula driven categorical aid programs, the distribution of which is determined by a variety of educational need-based formulas, categorical lump sum grants and "special categorical projects" (so-called "members' initiatives," or "bullet-aid" grant programs).

About 95 percent of total state aid is accounted for by formula-driven general operating and categorical aids and is incorporated into computer runs which determine their size and distribution. For example, for school year 1990-91 they amounted to $8.5 billion out of total state aid of $8.9 billlion. Grant programs and other aid categories accounted for another $454 million. (See Table 6.)

The huge proportion of monies allocated to operating aid and other formula programs would appear to leave very little money available for any other significant purpose. However, that "very little" is manipulated and distributed in a manner calculated to gain maximum political impact. During the various stages of budget negotiation, categorical grant programs are used to cajole and assuage those members who represent those districts that will lose money as a result of the way in which the formula-driven operating and categorical aids are being distributed. Special attention is given to the needs of these members. Decisions regarding these grants are made known prior to the formation of the majority party consensus. Commitments by the leadership of favored treatment for these members are an important part to the binding that makes agreement possible in the conference majority of each house. Those members whose districts stand to lose as a result of the distribution of formula aids vote for budget approval knowing that they will be somewhat compensated by a favored share of categorical grants.

Another, although smaller, form of member compensations is the manner in which special categorical projects—so-called members' items—are distributed. Although total funds for these purposes amounted to only $12 million in 1990-91 (see Table 6), this form of aid nevertheless plays a central role in the budget process. But its distribution only comes after the fact. These monies are set aside in both the assembly and senate as a lump sum for special programs in local school districts. The individual grants are often quite small, sometimes as low as $2,000.

These special grants are awarded during the process of negotiation in party conference, or to assuage resentment on the part of those who feel that their districts are being shortchanged. Usually, decisions regarding the distribution of these grants are made known prior to the formation of the majority party consensus. Sometimes, they are dispensed much later, at the conclusion of the budgetary process. Anticipation and expectation of these grants are an important leadership tool in securing support of members.

As small as these sums may be, they are still of critical importance to legislators. Their special nature assures a high degree of prominence and visibility to the legislator in the local community, where they are referred to as the special programs of the member. Local media also feature announcements of the program and enhance the member's visibility. Even in those years where little money is available for significant overall increases in educational aid, members eagerly seek these programs, so that they do not have to go back to their district empty handed. Therefore, in a manner unrelated to the amount of money involved, these programs are the final glue and cement, the guarantee of the seal of approval, that bind and put the finishing touches to the final legislative package.

The politics of school aid may be best understood as a series of actions, engaged in by the membership of the dominant party conference in each house of the legislature, to control and limit the effects of the basic operating-aid formula so that majority support can be garnered for the school aid bill. The operating aid formula, if left unimpeded to do its work, is the most equalizing part of the state school aid package. However, its effects are not politically acceptable unless special arrangements are made to take care of many of the legislators whose districts feel aggrieved.

Although member items have played a role in facilitating accommodation, over the long run the sums involved are not large enough to wield effective influence on coalition building. Hence, the development of new aids, for specific categorical purposes or for general supplemental support, that implement the logic of the politics of school aid, which is essentially a scheme to circumvent the equalizing impact of the general operating aid formula.

A more recent development, with potentially greater implications because of its increasing size, is the expansion of two new forms of state aid: supplemental support and high tax. As our previous discussion in Chapter 2 indicated, these aids have been devised in order to compensate for the diminishing returns accruing to wealthier districts from the variety of save-harmless formulas.

Supplemental support aid and high tax aid are new additions to the state aid package. In the few years since they were introduced, supplemental support has risen to $429.4 million and high tax to $218 million for 1990-91. (See Table 6.) Both types of aid also contain clauses that reduce amounts going to either the Big Five cities (supplemental support aid) or eliminate it entirely for New York City (high tax aid), thereby guaranteeing that more money will be directed to wealthier districts.

The Formula Mystique

> ... [p]roduced by a daunting and difficult finance system so onerous in its effect on districts poor in realty wealth (see 83 AD2d 217, especially pp. 223-226) and so complex in its application that Judge James D. Hopkins, concurring in the majority's finding that the State is violating the State Constitution's education article, felt called upon to complain that "the design of a uniform and harmonious system conceived by its nineteenth century authors had been frustrated and distorted" into "a veritable jungle of labyrinthine incongruity," an "Ossa of confusion piled on a Pelion of disorder."[10]

In Chapter 2, we described the manner in which attention has been focused since 1902 on the development of a state aid equalizing formula. Since that time, all major proposals for reform have focused on changing the formula as the key element in lessening disparities. With all the revisions and adaptations of the last half-century, the formula has taken on an existence of its own—complex, obscure and fathomable only to the few cognoscenti who have been immersed in its rites and rituals.

Max Rubin, chairman of the New York State Special Task Force on Equity and Excellence in Education, appointed by then Governor Hugh L. Carey and a major figure in school finance for the last thirty years, once stated that the school formula was so complex and arcane that he knew of only one person in the state who understood it: Lois Wilson, then the educational specialist in the State Budget Office. Mr. Rubin was exaggerating, but the implications of his statement are worth pondering. When a formula is so complex that it defies understanding, even by those engaged in formulating policy, the inevitable results are dependence and impotence on the part of the legislators and decision makers and increased reliance on the experts and the technicians called upon to manipulate the formula in order to achieve the goals agreed upon by the leadership and legislators.

In reality, more than one person understands the intricacies of the educational aid formula, but as one identifies these people there is an appreciation of the power of such knowledge and its use in the political process. The necessity to deal with the formula creates jobs and roles for professionals and technicians in the Education Committee and the Senate Finance Committee and the Assembly Ways and Means Committee. These are the people at the helm, representing the wishes of the leadership during the entire budgetary process, the constant source of information and interpretation about latest developments. Certainly they are not the captains of the process, for they can be dismissed or shifted at the will of the leadership. But the leaders are incapable of navigating by themselves and are usually dependent on the technicians for guidance and direction—a dependence often semantically disguised by references to the need for more data and printouts.

The complexity and obscurity of the formula play an important role in the budgetary and political process. Its mystique hallows its operations, removing it from knowledge and scrutiny by most of the actors. At the same time, it elevates staff to a level of power far beyond public awareness and comprehension. A few individuals who understand the process implement the leaders' and members' dictates in a manner not comprehensible to most of those involved, leaving the impression that the formula is driving the system in directions not controllable or responsive to the wishes of the leaders and the needs of the budgetary process. It is reliance on the formula mystique that camouflages the unfolding of events, imbuing results with an unchallangeable aura due to its emergence from the fount of scientific rationality and neutrality. Absent are the challenges and scrutiny usually given to subjects and actions more clearly perceived to be within the common realm of understanding.

During the various phases and cycles of the budget approval process, technicians and staff are called upon to settle on estimates, remedy discrepancies, and, when necessary, make adjustments that facilitate approval both within conferences and between the two houses. For that last phase, it is imperative that communications be kept open, if not between members of different parties, then certainly between their technical emissaries who push through the final agreements. Just one more formula adjustment, one more manipulation of a category, a few special adjustments on members' items—and printouts are revised, readied and once more distributed, with the final assent now almost certain. The closed and hidden nature of the process enhances the power of leaders to resist and negotiate demands while their technical staffs possess the knowledge to make "fixes." And throughout this long, tortuous process of negotiation, compromise and revision, the elusiveness of the aid formula plays a central role of camouflage and cover, concealing the details of deals, while allowing the general aura of harmony to take shape. Its very complexity facilitates the manipulations and arrangements generated in the political process.

Imperatives of the Political Process

> They come to Congress hoping to change the world, or at least a
> corner of it. They bring their ideals, their values and priorities, their
> vision of where the nation should be headed. But then they discover
> that almost everyone else has a vision too, and to get anything at all
> done, they must learn the art of compromise.

> ... Members nevertheless discover that most issues involve grada-
> tion, rather than simple right and wrong. In addition, Congressional
> leaders are adept at packaging legislation that has something for
> everyone, producing hard choices for committed members.[11]

While our concern has been to render the legislative process more
intelligible, our focus remains on the issue of equality of educational
opportunity and the effect that these events have on the likelihood of
achieving that goal, or at the very least of significantly reducing existing disparities. On the basis of the above presentation, the future augurs
poorly for any hope of significant amelioration. Certainly there are a
number of factors of differing and varying effect that make it difficult
to foretell results with precision. But the underlying structure seems
certain to dictate limited significant change.

The structure of political institutions and the political process forces events into a mold that undermines attempts to reform the system
in the direction of greater equality. This despite the great promises and
hopes that equality advocates have attached to their efforts during the
great struggles since the turn of the century.

Equality is a goal, the justice of which is regularly proclaimed by
governors, legislative leaders, the educational community and, even
more piously, by the many special commissions and task forces that are
created to study and propose. But all these utterances are drowned out
by the onslaught of politics and power, mere platitudes before the
realities of the legislative process, to be discarded by necessities of
political compromise and budgetary approval.

Our brief survey of politics and power in New York State indicates
that progress toward equalization is retarded by the rules of the game
discussed earlier. Of course, conditions vary from year to year, and one
might argue that a significant expansion of state aid would allow for the
satisfaction of both goals—the best of both worlds—taking care of
member needs and also paying attention to the equality issue. However,
this perspective focuses solely on the state role, leaving out the possibility that more affluent districts may increase their local tax rates

while less affluent areas might reduce theirs as a result of increased state aid.

Without placing a cap on local tax efforts, or enforcing maintenance of effort provisions on all districts, it is unlikely that state aid by itself can achieve the goal of equality, especially since its share, even with the recent large state increases, is only about 43 percent of total educational expenditures. Therefore, one can only conclude that the issue of equality will remain a perennial part of legislative debate and conflict, as constant as the preservation of distance between the vision and the reality of equal educational opportunity.

Seeking Redress in the Courts

Inequality of educational opportunity has been an issue in almost all of the fifty states. Indeed, in many states the range of inequality is much greater than in New York State. In many of the older northern and eastern states, the political struggle to achieve equality has a history reaching back to the nineteenth century. The historical record of struggle and failure brought frustration and dismay to those who sought change through the traditional mechanisms of the political process. It was recognized that the political process has imbedded within it the very elements that set the boundaries limiting the achievement of significant change.

In the American system, frustration and dismay with the political process often leads to court challenges as an appeal of last resort. This has been the case in many areas of social and political turmoil, and education has an especially long history in this regard. The 1960s, more than any other period in recent American history, was a time when judicial channels were flooded with appeals for change and redress over matters that were being blocked by the political process. The issue of equality of educational opportunity provoked litigation in many state courts as well as the U.S. Supreme Court. In Chapter 4, we trace the chain of events that resulted in a challenge to the constitutionality of the New York State system of educational finance, discuss issues that were similarly raised in many other states and also assess the potency of a judicial challenge to a set of events that seemed irreparable through the political process.

NOTES

1. Most of the material in this chapter, concerning the politics of educational finance in New York State, is based on personal interviews. These interviews involved many important figures engaged in the formulation and implementation of educational policy. We are most appreciative to all of these persons for their time, attention and cooperation. It would not have been possible for us to develop this work without their aid, since the subject we are discussing is known only to those who are directly engaged in its operations.
2. Testimony of Dr. Arvid Burke in *Board of Education, Levittown Union Free School District v. Nyquist*, 96 Misc. 2d 466 (Trial Transcript, pp. 10925-26).
3. *Annual Educational Summary, 1988-1989* (Albany: New York State Education Department, 1989), Table 57, pp. 70-92.
4. *New York Times,* editorial, March 26, 1986.
5. Jerry Miner, "A Decade of New York State Aid to Local Schools," Occasional Paper No. 141, Metropolitan Studies Program, Syracuse University, September 1990, Table 10, p. 28.
6. Edward B. Fiske, "New York: Equalization = Irony + Dilemma; Finding Funds for Schools Isn't Easy," *New York Times,* February 11, 1979.
7. Manly Fleischmann, "School Financing and State Governance," in *State of New York Task Force on Aid to Education* (Report to Governor Hugh L. Carey), Albany, N.Y., April 1975, p. 53.
8. Our information on the population and composition of assembly and senate districts is derived from the data base of the New York State Legislative Task Force on Demographics Research and Reapportionment. These extensive data are used in Chapter 5 for our analysis of the school district composition of Democratic assembly districts outside New York City, and are also used for our conclusions in this chapter about the political impact of school districts upon legislative voting patterns.
9. All information for 1987-88 derived from "Preliminary Description of 1987-88 New York State School Aid Programs," Education Unit, New York State Division of Budget, Albany, N.Y., April 30, 1987.
10. Dissenting opinion of Judge Jacob O. Fuchsberg in *Board of Education, Levittown Union Free School District v. Nyquist*, 57

N.Y. 2d 27, 55 (1983), citing concurring opinion of Judge James D. Hopkins, 83 A.D. 2d 217, 269 (1981).
11. Martin Tolchin, "Congress: What Became of Those Ideals, or Those Idealists?" *New York Times,* August 7, 1984, p. B6.

4.

TURNING TO THE COURTS

The life of the law has not been logic: it has been experience. The felt necessities of the time, the prevalent moral and political theories, intuitions of public policy, avowed or unconscious, even the prejudices which judges share with their fellow-men, have had a good deal more to do than the syllogism in determining the rules by which men should be governed. The law embodies the story of a nation's development through many centuries, and it cannot be dealt with as if it contained only the axioms and corollaries of a book of mathematics.

—Oliver Wendell Holmes

* * *

We are under a Constitution, but the Constitution is what the judges say it is.

—Charles Evans Hughes

Beginning with Cubberly in the first decade of the twentieth century,[1] educational finance reformers have sought to equalize the distribution of resources for education. However, as discussed in Chapter 3, the dynamics of legislative politics, economic reality and human nature have combined to thwart progress toward this goal. Efforts to obtain judicial intervention in the area of educational finance reforms reached a peak in the 1960s and 1970s at the same time as, to paraphrase Archibald Cox, "the genie of equal protection was let out of the bottle." The constitutional doctrine of equal protection became the principal weapon in the struggle for reform, providing the basis for numerous court challenges to state educational finance systems.

Constitutional Theory and Educational Finance

The early 1960s was a time of revolutionary growth in the development of equal protection doctrine. A series of judicial decisions, most notably in the field of criminal procedure, established, in the view of many, the principle that states have an affirmative duty to compensate for disadvantages flowing from differences in economic circumstances. Inevitably, reformers sought to extend this principle to other aspects of life.[2]

Arthur E. Wise, in his doctoral dissertation at the University of Chicago,[3] first propounded the argument that the equal protection revolution should be expanded to include educational finance. He maintained that education is a state function and that no child should have fewer resources devoted to his education because of economic circumstances. Implicit in Wise's argument was the notion that children should be equally educated, even if that meant that some children had to be given more attention than others for this to occur. To the extent this notion encompassed the idea of compensatory education, it would soon run afoul of the "manageable standards" requirement first laid down in the case of *McInnis v. Shapiro.*[4]

McInnis v. Shapiro was the prototype of school finance lawsuits that would be instigated during the 1960s and 1970s. Both the nature of plaintiff's grievances and the structure of the state's school system, in this case the State of Illinois, were typical of those that followed. Each school district in Illinois raised school revenues by imposing a tax on the real property within the district. Illinois, like most other states, supplemented the locally raised monies by means of "foundation grants" originally designed to equalize per-pupil expenditure levels. The basis of the lawsuit was that the same local tax effort in different school districts yielded different amounts of revenues, because of the different values of the real property in districts. The complaint also alluded to the problem of variations in local tax rates and revenues resulting from such factors as local differences in income, other local governmental financial demands and local attitudes toward need for quality education. The relief sought was to have Illinois assume the burden of financing public education so as to assure that each child, upon completion of schooling, would be equally prepared to assume his place in society. The argument was rejected by a three-judge federal district court as a "nebulous concept" that "provided no discoverable and manageable standards by which a court can determine when the Constitution is satisfied and when it is violated." The United States Supreme Court affirmed summarily, without full briefs, oral argument or written opinion.

To circumvent the requirement of "manageable standards," John E. Coons, William H. Clune and Stephen D. Sugarman[5] constructed a constitutional theory that conceptually avoided the necessity of formulating judicially manageable standards for the determination of educational needs. They posited the principle that "the quality of public education may not be a function of wealth other than the wealth of the state as a whole." As one means of implementing this principle, they offered a district power equalizing scheme under which the state would guarantee that for any locally determined property tax rate the district would receive a fixed number of dollars per student regardless of the district's tax base. Thus, a local school district would continue to retain the autonomy to determine its own expenditure level not as a function of district real property wealth, but rather only as a function of the district's willingness to tax itself.

Although fiscal neutrality, as this theory is known, is an extremely innovative and powerful theory of constitutional law, it was found substantively wanting by many school reformers because it did not assure equality of expenditure, only equality of revenues from similar tax effort. Consequently, other reformers advanced the theory of a constitutionally required adequate educational opportunity. This theory argues that there is some identifiable quantum of education that a state is required to furnish to each school child. These two theories have produced different and sometimes diametrically opposite results when tested in state courts. (The twenty-five cases decided by state high courts are categorized in Table 10.)

Standards of Equal Protection in Review

Challenges to existing school finance schemes have alleged that they deny equal protection of the law, which is guaranteed by the Fourteenth Amendment to the United States Constitution and corresponding provisions of the various state constitutions. To explore the issues involved in school finance litigation, a brief review of equal protection doctrine is necessary. Equal protection cases involve disparity of treatment based on governmental (legislative or administrative) classifications. The critical issue is whether the different treatment inherent in a classification scheme constitutes invidious discrimination in violation of the equal protection clause. To make this determination, the judiciary employs one of three standards of review.

The traditional or "rational basis" standard of review requires only that there be a rational relationship between the act complained of and a legitimate governmental purpose. Thus, only totally arbitrary classifications will be struck down under the traditional test. A more stringent standard, the strict scrutiny test, applies when the court finds that the challenged classification interferes with a fundamental right or involves a suspect classification. In such a case, the classification is unconstitutional unless it is necessary for the achievement of a compelling state interest. Voting rights, many criminal procedure rights, the right to travel, the right to procreate, the right of marital and family privacy and First Amendment rights, such as freedom of speech, religion and association, have been held by the Supreme Court to be fundamental. Race and religion have been universally recognized by the courts as suspect classifications.

In practice, equal protection analysis almost always turns on which test is applied. Use of the traditional rational basis test typically results in upholding the classification, while application of the strict scrutiny test will usually invalidate a challenged classification. Dissatisfaction with the rigidity of the two-tier analysis has led some legal scholars and courts to advocate a more flexible, stronger rational basis test.[6]

Under this intermediate test, a legislative classification must bear more than a mere rational relationship to a legitimate legislative purpose. It would have to substantially further the legislative purpose. This so-called "heightened scrutiny" standard focuses on the relationship between the legislative end sought to be achieved and the legislative classification adopted as a means to that end. It has generally been applied in cases where the interests affected were sensitive but did not involve fundamental rights or suspect classifications. All three of these standards of equal protection review have appeared in school finance decisions. As would be expected, litigants seeking to strike down existing laws have sought either to have education declared a fundamental right, to have wealth declared a suspect classification, or—at a minimum—to have the heightened scrutiny standard applied.

Equal Protection Challenges

Educational reformers and legal scholars, seeking to commence what they considered would be an historic lawsuit, decided on John Serrano, a Los Angeles social worker and father of a school-age child, and the California educational finance system as the ideal test vehicles. Many activists, reformers and scholars contributed to the plaintiff's legal theories.

Evidence adduced at trial illustrated the vast disparities among neighboring school districts in amount spent per pupil, irrespective of local taxing effort. For example, in the wealthy Beverly Hills district, $1,231.72 was spent per pupil with a tax rate of only $2.38, while in the poorer, nearby Baldwin Park district, a tax rate of well over $5.00 yielded a per-pupil expenditure of less than half as much, despite the infusion of a higher amount of state aid. Plaintiffs argued that education, being necessary for the exercise of constitutionally guaranteed rights, is itself a "fundamental right," that access to education cannot be conditioned on wealth and that discrimination in access to education based on residence in one or another school district created a "suspect classification." If these views were to be accepted, such discrimination could not stand in the absence of showing a compelling state interest.

The landmark decision of the California Supreme Court in *Serrano I*[7] was the first major decision by a high court invalidating a state's school finance system on the basis of equal protection. The court specifically held education to be a fundamental right under both the state and the federal constitutions and wealth to be a suspect classification. The court articulated its conclusions as follows:

> The California public school financing system, as presented to us by the plaintiff's complaint supplemented by matters judicially noticed, since it deals intimately with education, obviously touches on a fundamental interest. For the reasons we have explained in detail, this system conditions the full entitlement to such interest on wealth, classifies its recipients on the basis of their collective affluence and makes the quality of a child's education depend upon the resources of his school district and ultimately upon the pocketbook of his parents. We find that such a financing system as presently constituted is not necessary to the attainment of any compelling state interest. Since it does not withstand the requisite "strict scrutiny," it denies to the plaintiffs and others similarly situated the equal protection of the laws. If the allegations of the complaint are sustained, the financial system must fall and the statutes comprising it must be found unconstitutional.[8]

Since *Serrano I* only involved the legal sufficiency of plaintiff's complaint, the case was sent back to the trial court for an evidentiary hearing. However, before trial commenced, the United States Supreme Court handed down a decision affecting the entire complexion of school finance litigation. *San Antonio Independent School District v. Rodriguez*[9] disposed of the equal protection clause of the federal constitution as a basis for school finance lawsuits.

In that case, Mexican-American parents of children attending public schools in an urban school district in San Antonio instituted a class action on behalf of school children throughout the state who were members of minorities, or who were poor and resided in school districts having a low property tax base. Plaintiffs challenged Texas' statutory system of financing public school education, claiming discriminatory educational treatment and a denial of federal equal protection because public schools in each school district were funded in part by revenues realized from property taxes collected within the respective school districts.

The Texas system had historically relied on a combination of local property tax revenues and state funds to finance its public schools. Substantial disparities existed in the value of assessable property located in the state's different school districts. Texas maintained a minimum foundation program, which required the state and the local subdivisions to contribute to a fund for basic current expenses. While the minimum foundation program was intended to "equalize" the educational tax burden among the school districts, it did not significantly ameliorate disparities in interdistrict per-pupil wealth and expenditures. Moreover, each locality was permitted to supplement the foundation level program through an *ad valorem* tax on its property.

The Supreme Court declined to apply a strict scrutiny analysis to the Texas system, finding neither a suspect classification nor a fundamental constitutional right. The Court found that the Texas financing system did not result in the absolute deprivation of an education to any definable category of the poor and that "a large, diverse, and amorphous class, unified only by the common factor of residence in districts that happen to have less taxable wealth than other districts" lacked the traditional indicia of "suspectness" necessary to trigger strict scrutiny equal protection analysis. Justice Powell, writing for the majority, observed that the equal protection clause was intended to protect individuals, not governmental units (property-poor school districts), from discriminatory state action. Since plaintiffs could not prove a statistically valid relationship between poor people and property-poor school districts, there was no suspect classification of people based on wealth. Moreover, Justice Powell pointed out that the Court had "never heretofore held that wealth discrimination alone provides an adequate basis for invoking strict scrutiny."

In addition, the Court held that determining whether the right to an education could be deemed "fundamental" for purposes of applying the equal protection clause was not accomplished by measuring the importance of the activity, but depended upon whether the right was "explicitly or implicitly" guaranteed by the federal constitution. The majority opinion held that "the undisputed importance of education will not alone cause this Court to depart from the usual standard for reviewing a state's social and economic legislation." Finding no such guarantee in the federal constitution, the Court upheld the Texas public school finance system.

The Court was also concerned about the effect any other result would have on the distribution of other public services. The majority opinion observed that "the logical limitation on appellee's nexus theory are difficult to perceive. How, for instance, is education to be distinguished from the significant personal interests in the basics of decent food and shelter?" The Court finally concluded that the system, with its reliance on local wealth, was rationally related to the state purpose of assuring a basic education for every child in the state, while permitting and encouraging a large measure of participation in and control of each district's schools at the local level.

In his vigorous dissent, Justice Marshall observed that "nothing in the Court's decision today should inhibit further review of state educational funding schemes under state constitutional provisions." The California Supreme Court responded to this invitation in *Serrano II*.[10] That court rejected the argument that *Rodriguez* had undercut its reliance on equal protection, and reaffirmed its earlier decision by holding education to be a fundamental right and wealth a suspect classification under California's constitution, without reference to the federal constitution.

The Supreme Court's decision in *Rodriguez*, by eliminating reliance on the equal protection clause of the United States Constitution, had the obvious effect of redirecting all school finance litigation into the state courts. As has been previously mentioned, state courts have not been consistent in their equal protection analysis of school finance laws under the various state constitutions. The diversity of constitutional provisions being construed, differing views on the fundamental nature of the right to education (and opposite views on whether wealth is a suspect classification) have inevitably led to inconsistent results. Of the twenty-five state high courts that have decided the issue as of the end of 1990, ten have invalidated their state's traditional school finance laws and fifteen have upheld them. (See Table 10.)

New York State Equal Protection Challenge Fails

While the California Supreme Court departed from the federal equal protection holding in *Rodriguez* by relying on its state equal protection clause to strike down the state school finance system, the New York Court of Appeals, the state's high court, reached an opposite result in the *Levittown* case.[11] In addition to the "usual" issues raised in school finance cases, the New York litigation introduced the hitherto unexplored concept of municipal overburden.

The Fleischmann Commission, appointed by Governor Nelson A. Rockefeller in 1969, had issued a three-volume report documenting inequalities throughout the state in authoritative detail. A gubernatorial task force appointed by Governor Rockefeller's successor, Malcolm Wilson, had come to the same conclusion—that existing school finance inequities were intolerable. When legislative inaction continued, this litigation arose. The original plaintiffs in *Levittown,* the school boards of twenty-seven property-poor rural and suburban school districts, plus a number of school children and their parents, commenced the action in 1974. Their complaint charged that the nexus between local property wealth and school expenditures, and the resulting inequalities in educational opportunity and quality, violated the equal protection clause of the federal constitution, as well as the education article and equal protection clause of the New York State Constitution. The inequities complained of were already well known to all. Levittown had a real property wealth of $22,731 per pupil and levied a tax of 32.33 mills, while neighboring Great Neck had $95,944 of real property per pupil and levied a tax of only 25.51 mills. Even with its greater tax effort and the addition of a larger amount of state aid, Levittown could spend only $1,443 per pupil, while Great Neck spent $2,667 per pupil. The four largest city school districts in the state—New York, Buffalo, Rochester and Syracuse—quickly joined in the *Levittown* suit as plaintiffs-intervenors. These districts, which were not low-wealth districts but were revealed by the task force to have low per-pupil expenditure, alleged that the state school finance system discriminated against them by failing to take into account their special needs and higher costs—their so-called municipal overburden.

Between April 1976 and January 1977, Justice L. Kingsley Smith presided over a one hundred twenty-two-day trial. In the fullest exploration of a school finance system ever conducted in a courtroom, some one hundred twenty-eight witnesses, four hundred trial exhibits and 23,000 pages of trial testimony documented what everyone already knew. The trial judge held, in more than four hundred discrete findings, that New York's school finance scheme discriminated among districts on the basis of local property wealth and that the legislature had allowed hundreds of unevenly endowed districts to bear the principal burden of supporting their own schools. Property-rich districts like Scarsdale and Great Neck enjoyed the luxury of fashioning and implementing educational policies of their own choice, thanks to their abundant local resources. Property-poor districts, on the other hand, had to make do with less. In addition to local tax revenues, school districts also received funds from the state treasury. While some of these amounts, such as those allocated on a per-pupil basis, had an equalizing effect, others, such as those resulting from save-harmless provisions and other forms of legislative largess, merely increased the disparity between districts. Rather than formulate and pursue their own educational policies, property-poor districts had been reduced to a kind of educational triage or desperate annual determinations as to which programs to cut, what teachers and other staff to let go and which necessary tools to do without.

After extensive post-trial briefing, Justice Smith rendered a decision on June 23, 1978, holding that New York's school finance scheme violated both the federal and state constitutions.[12] In his extensive findings of fact, which were keyed to the trial record, the trial judge found that rich districts spent more money per pupil than poor districts, that they did so with a lower tax effort and that they used the more ample funds to buy more education resources and to offer a substantially higher level of educational opportunity to their children. He found that even the allegedly equalizing provisions of the school finance formula failed to correct these inequities and that in many respects they exacerbated them. Accordingly, Justice Smith held that the state failed to provide "all the state's school children the opportunity to acquire at least those basic skills necessary to function in a democratic society," and thereby denied them equal protection. In response to the separate federal claim of plaintiffs-intervenors that municipal overburden created another type of invidious discrimination, he found the overall financing scheme to be "irrational."

Justice Smith determined that his legal conclusions were reachable under either the strict scrutiny or heightened scrutiny standards of review, thereby rejecting the argument that such inequities were the price that must be paid in order to preserve and promote "local control." In so ruling, he relied upon testimony from the state's own witnesses that the existing education financing laws were in fact inconsistent with local control and that reforms could be made without sacrificing that objective.

The *Levittown* trial court was the first court in the nation to hold that the concept of municipal overburden was a factor to be considered in assessing a state's school aid formula. For the purpose of providing "equalizing" aid to school districts, New York's statute measured local capacity to finance schools by the value of local real property and income behind each of the district's students. This approach assumes that school districts throughout the state are equally able to draw upon their tax base for school funds. Justice Smith found that assumption to be false, because essential non-education services of city districts inexorably drained local revenues, reducing sharply those districts' ability to finance public education from local taxable resources. The court based this finding on extensive testimony and documentary evidence establishing the need in large cities for expanded services, such as police and fire protection, public assistance, health, correction facilities and housing, as well as for some services like mass transit not provided by smaller communities. The financial burdens created by old housing stock, deteriorating municipal facilities, a disproportionate population of poor and uneducated individuals and the overall economic decline of the cities were also considered. In the view of the court, cities' unparalleled expenditures and tax levies for non-school purposes created a "fiscal imbalance" and prevented a city district "from devoting a normal proportion of its fiscal resources for education."

The court found that while jurisdictions outside New York's four largest cities were able to spend 45 percent of their local taxes for schools, the cities could spend only 28 percent. Measured in per capita terms, non-education outlays were much higher in the four cities than in the surrounding counties and the rest of the state; in New York City, $401.06 was the per capita non-educational expenditure from local revenue, whereas only $183.17 was spent per capita in the rest of the state as a whole. The court concluded that "New York's aid formula overstates the cities' capacity to finance their schools" by disregarding "the 'municipal overburden' drain of non-educational services on the local tax dollar." Failure to take municipal overburden into account was held to render the state aid formula unconstitutionally discriminatory.

On appeal, the second department of the appellate division, affirmed that portion of the trial court's holding which was grounded on state constitutional provisions, applying the intermediate or heightened scrutiny standard to invalidate the state educational finance system.[13] However, the appellate court reversed the trial court's holdings with respect to federal equal protection claims on the authority of *Rodriguez;* this reversal also disposed of plaintiffs-intervenors' claims based on municipal overburden.

While *Levittown* was proceeding through the state appellate courts, still another gubernatorial task force was appointed to examine the statutory scheme and to fashion alternatives to recommend to the legislature in the event the decision was affirmed. The report of the Special Task Force on Equity and Excellence in Education (the "Rubin Commission") was submitted to Governor Hugh L. Carey on February 1, 1982. In forwarding the report, chairman Max Rubin wrote to the governor, "Of course, we do not know what the outcome as to constitutionality will be in the Court of Appeals. But we do know that serious inequities exist in the present formula."[14]

The three-volume study confirmed the findings of the trial court that gross disparities existed in the statutory scheme, that local property wealth was the chief source of differences in spending among districts and that rich districts used their more abundant resources to provide greater opportunities for their children than was possible in property-poor districts. The commission agreed with the intermediate appellate court that the passage of time since Justice Smith's decision had only exacerbated these problems and made the need for reform more compelling.

At about the same time, Governor Carey, in his February 17, 1982, education message to the legislature, urged:

> New York State must act now to redress the inequities inherent in its school aid formula. . . . Today, the financial inequalities in education are more pronounced than at any time in the State's history.

> The divergence in spending between wealthy and poor districts increases annually, with the taxpayers in poorer districts facing intolerable, escalating property taxes.

> New York must stop the unfairness and inequity in the financing of education. We need to demonstrate to all New Yorkers that our great state clearly stands for equality in educational opportunity.

That was not to be. On June 23, 1982, the New York Court of Appeals reversed the decisions below, rejecting both state and federal constitutional claims. The court accepted the elaborate and carefully documented findings of the trial judge, and the majority agreed that:

> [I]t must be recognized that there are . . . significant inequalities in the availability of financial support for local school districts, ranging from minor discrepancies to major differences, resulting in significant unevenness in the educational opportunities offered. These disparities may properly be ascribed in some respects to the wide variances between the property assessment bases on which local district taxes are imposed.[15]

Nevertheless, the state's high court rejected the federal equal protection claim, on the ground that such a claim had been "considered and rejected by the Supreme Court of the United States" in *Rodriguez.* The state court held that "the conclusions reached in that case dictate a similar result in the present litigation" with respect to equal protection arguments based on the state constitution. Specifically, the court adopted the use of a rational basis test, rather than one based on heightened or strict scrutiny, because, like the Supreme Court, it found "that the justification offered by the State—the preservation and promotion of local control of education—is both a legitimate State interest and one to which the present financing system is reasonably related."

Underlying Concerns About Judicial Intervention

It is believed that the New York Court of Appeals' decision was influenced significantly by concern that a contrary result could involve the state's courts in the legislative-executive budgetary process, making expenditure and tax decisions not only with respect to education but, ultimately, other areas of public service as well. There are several sources for this belief.

Prior to *Levittown,* the court had expressed such concerns in *Donohue v. Copiague Union Free School District.*[16] In that case, which dealt with the issue of educational malpractice in the schools of the state, the court held that an action for educational malpractice would not be cognizable in the courts as a matter of public policy. The rationale for such holding was that control and management of educational affairs had been vested in the New York State Board of Regents and the Commissioner of Education; in the court's view, the judiciary should not interfere with such affairs. In his concurring opinion, Judge (now Chief Judge) Sol Wachtler was even more adamant, arguing that a cause of action sounding in educational malpractice should not be recognized at all, because the practical problems of establishing reasonably manageable standards would be so formidable.

These concerns could only have been heightened when the court considered *Levittown* since that case involved an additional actor–the legislature. As demonstrated in Chapter 3, fine-tuning of the educational state aid formula occurs each year as part of New York's legislative budgetary process. The court may well have been wary of becoming a super-legislative body with the obligation of overseeing this process each year. If more money was needed for certain educational programs in poorer districts, where would the money come from? The legislature's choices are manifold, but for the judiciary to be involved in requiring or approving those choices could be seen as a usurpation of legislative prerogative and a negation of the doctrine of separation of powers. The court observed that because the allocation of public funds "are matters peculiarly appropriate for formulation by the legislative body . . . we would be reluctant to override those decisions by mandating an even higher priority for education in the absence, possibly, of gross and glaring inadequacy—something not shown to exist in consequence of the present school financing system."[17] In 1991, some nine years after the New York Court of Appeals' *Levittown* decision, a group of twenty Long Island school districts accepted the court's implied invitation to attempt to demonstrate "gross and glaring inadequacy" in New York's school financing.[18] The plaintiffs alleged that in the years since *Levittown* the per-student disparity in spending between the ten poorest Long Island districts and the average Long Island district had quadrupled to about $1,600 from $400. In addition, the per-student spending gap between the poorest and the wealthiest district on Long Island had risen even more to about $5,000. Statewide, the discrepancies were even starker. Some districts in Westchester County spent $30,000 per student in the 1989-90 school year, while others in rural Alleghany County spent barely $5,000. These expenditure differences clearly flow from the vast disparities in district property wealth. For example, in Suffolk County the average property valuation per student was $297,335. The extremes ranged from $82,980 in the William Floyd District to 10.3 million dollars in the adjoining Quogue School District. Whether these discrepancies will equate to a "gross and glaring inadequacy" in the eyes of the New York courts will probably not be decided for another few years.

Prior to the court's decision in *Levittown,* Max Rubin, in his capacity as chairman of the Special Task Force on Equity and Excellence in Education, had argued that it would be impossible for the courts to manage an education finance formula on a day-to-day basis. He believed that this approach would immerse the courts in the nitty gritty of educational administration as well as the legislative-executive budgetary process. He stated on many occasions, including in interviews with the authors and a lecture at Hunter College, that this was the main reason for his belief that a legislative, not judicial, solution was both necessary and desirable on a permanent basis.

An opposite view was expressed by Court of Appeals Judge Jacob Fuchsberg, the dissenting judge in *Levittown.* He maintained in an interview with the authors that an order of the court directing the legislature to fashion an acceptable scheme would be obeyed, by coercive power if need be. He referred with approval to the actions of the New Jersey Supreme Court after it issued a judgment *(Robinson VI)*[19] which, in effect, required the New Jersey legislature to enact a new educational finance formula necessitating the appropriation of considerable additional monies. After lengthy debate, the New Jersey legislature was deadlocked by lack of agreement on a new funding source and the court, in frustration, ordered that after June 30, 1976, no monies could be expended to operate any public elementary or secondary school in the state until the legislature complied with its judgment. After a short one-week closure of the schools in July, affecting summer schools and playground activities, the legislature capitulated and voted a new educational formula with a new source of income—a state income tax. Thus, Judge Fuchsberg believed that a court could enter an order and, through its coercive powers, require the other branches of government to comply.

Both the Rubin and Fuchsberg scenarios are correct and even compatible with one another. However, they are based on different time frames. The coercive powers of the courts can accomplish change in an educational funding formula, as was demonstrated in New Jersey. However, over the long term it would be impossible for a court to maintain the equity it achieved with any such order. That equity is dependent upon factors—such as real property wealth, taxpayer income, residential settlement patterns and socioeconomic movements—which change over the years. Therefore, the courts would not be able to maintain a continuingly equitable formula without repeatedly substituting itself for legislative or educational officials in a process of "never-final" decisions. The New York Court of Appeals by its 6 to 1 vote, with Judge

Fuchsberg dissenting, chose not to become involved in the ongoing fiscal management of the school system. The implicit concern—that there are no manageable standards for the operation of a school finance system—harkens back to the prototype case of *McInnis v. Shapiro* (page 71).

In addition to theoretical constructs, empirical evidence also exists to support both views. The subsequent history of Serrano illustrates the validity of concerns about the difficulty of establishing manageable standards and the likelihood of permanent involvement of the judiciary in enforcing and monitoring compliance with the requirement for equalization. In *Serrano II,* the California Supreme Court affirmed the trial court's retention of continuing jurisdiction over the case for the purpose of affording relief to plaintiffs. In 1980, plaintiffs filed a petition to enforce the earlier judgment, alleging that the state had failed to remedy the wealth-related disparities between school districts in per-pupil expenditures, disparities which the original trial court had ordered to be reduced within six years to "considerably less than $100 per pupil." At a lengthy evidentiary hearing, the court took into account the intervening passage of Proposition 13, which had drastically limited available revenues from real property taxation. In order to prevent Proposition 13 from crippling the California school finance system, the legislature had significantly altered the system, effectively moving it toward a fully state-funded system. At the time of the hearing, the State of California funded 88 percent of total school expenditures. After increasing the $100 maximum permitted disparity to $198 because of inflation, 93 percent of the pupils (based on average daily attendance) were within the permissible range.

After accepting the foregoing evidence, the court held that the California system was no longer constitutionally defective, despite the fact that the school aid formula still reflected prior district real property values and tax rates. It seems inevitable that this type of judicial oversight will become a permanent feature of the school finance system in California, with the court deciding the maximum range of disparity that will not offend the California Constitution. Continued judicial involvement in two other states, New Jersey and West Virginia, is described later in this chapter.

In support of those who believe that, despite the dangers of continuing involvement, courts can and should become actively involved, it must be recognized that the two most fundamental changes in American society occurring in the second half of this century have resulted not from legislative or administrative action, but rather from

the intervention of the judiciary. There are certain inequities so inter-
woven with the psychological status, economic well-being and social
fabric of the people that elected representatives are paralyzed to act out
of fear of electoral reprisal. This is especially so when the inequity rests
mainly on the shoulders of the underprivileged and politically power-
less. The circumstances surrounding segregated schools and voting
malapportionment and the evils thereof were well understood for
decades, but relief came only from the courts in *Brown* v. *Board of
Education*[20] and *Baker* v. *Carr*.[21] Proponents of judicial intervention
further argue that, as society becomes accustomed to such judicially
mandated changes and after a few years of experience, subsequent administration will be taken on by the legislative and executive branches.
Obviously, the decision as to which approach will be taken and which
will prove more beneficial to American society is an issue that lies at
the heart of our form of democracy.

The State Constitution's Education Clause

In addition to the equal protection argument, the New York Court
of Appeals rejected the plaintiffs' claim in *Levittown* that the school
finance system violated the education clause of the state constitution.
Section 1 of Article XI of the New York State Constitution states that
"the legislature shall provide for the maintenance and support of a system of free common schools, wherein all the children of this state may
be educated."

The majority interpreted this provision to require only "[a] statewide system assuring minimum acceptable facilities and services" and
"a sound basic education." The court rather casually held that the standard was met in New York simply because the state's average per pupil
expenditure was greater than that in every other state but two. However,
the question of whether students are receiving a "sound basic education" may yet allow for further judicial challenge in other states, even
where the highest court has ruled that there is no violation of the state
equal protection clause. To develop this issue, we must consider how
courts in other states have dealt with the particular formulation of the
education clause in each state constitution.

In most states with a constitutional education clause, challenges to
the educational finance system have generally been two-pronged,
claiming violations of federal and state equal protection clauses as well
as the education clause of the state constitution. The exact nature of the
argument has varied, depending on the precise wording of the state's

education clause, but the essence of this phase of the litigation has been that the state constitution mandates a certain quality, quantity or minimum level of education and that some students were not receiving that constitutionally mandated level of education.

A framework for the analysis of state constitutional education clauses may be modeled on the experience of New Jersey. The New Jersey Supreme Court found in *Robinson I*[22] that New Jersey's school financing system did not violate either the federal or state equal protection clauses, but that it violated the mandate of the New Jersey Constitution requiring "a thorough and efficient system of free public schools." The court held that "[a] system of instruction in any district of the State which is not thorough and efficient falls short of the Constitutional command." However, the court went on to point out that New Jersey had never defined or spelled out the standard by which to judge whether any particular educational opportunity was thorough and efficient. The legislature responded to the decision in *Robinson I* by enacting a statute that explicitly set forth the goal of a thorough and efficient system of education and the principle elements of which it must consist:

> The goal of a thorough and efficient system of free public schools shall be to provide to all children in New Jersey, regardless of socioeconomic status or geographic location, the educational opportunity which will prepare them to function politically, economically and socially in a democratic society.[23]

The statute set forth the "major elements" to "serve as guidelines for the achievement of the legislative goal"; these included establishment of educational goals, instruction to produce the attainment of reasonable levels of proficiency in basic skills, adequate facilities, qualified personnel and monitoring at both the state and local levels. The State Commissioner of Education was statutorily empowered to determine whether a particular system of public education met the legislative standard for a thorough and efficient education. Later, the New Jersey Supreme Court in its decision known as *Robinson V*[24] held this scheme to be facially constitutional provided it would be fully funded.

Finally, after experiencing *Robinson I* through *V* and breathing a deep sigh of relief that they had finally put the equity issue to rest, the New Jersey court system was confronted with a brand new lawsuit eight years after *Robinson I* was commenced. The new plaintiffs were from four urban school districts. They alleged that the passage of time had proved the facially constitutional equity achieved by *Robinson* and its progeny to be illusory and that it was necessary to go back to the statutory drafting tables once again. Camden's city schools spent $1,535 per pupil per year during the 1976-77 school year while nearby Cherry Hill, a well-to-do suburb, spent $1,677, or nine percent more. In 1984-85, after ten years of state school financing equalization aid, Camden spent $3,318 per pupil and Cherry Hill spent $4,645, or 29 percent more. Similar statistics were presented for the three other urban school districts. In a decision rendered in June of 1990,[25] the New Jersey Supreme Court acknowledged "that only in the light of experience can one ever come to know whether a particular program is achieving the desired end." The court then reviewed the "as applied" constitutionality of the school funding statute enacted by the legislature in response to *Robinson I*, which it had held to be facially constitutional in *Robinson V*. The court found that the fiscal disparities set out above led to disparities in the quality level of education (course offerings, teacher ratios and experience, and physical facilities) between the wealthier suburban districts and poorer urban districts.

> Disparity exists, therefore, between education in these poorer urban districts and that in the affluent suburban districts; it is severe and forms an independent basis for our finding of a lack of a thorough and efficient education in these poorer urban districts—these students simply cannot possibly enter the same market or the same society as their peers educated in wealthier districts.[26]

On the basis of the foregoing, the state supreme court held that New Jersey's school financing system was unconstitutional as applied to poorer urban school districts. The remedy it ordered was that the funding statute be amended to assure funding of education in poorer urban districts at the same level as in property-rich districts, and that such funding not depend on the ability of local school districts to tax, but must be mandated and guaranteed by the state. An amended statute, designed to conform to the court decision, was enacted by the New Jersey legislature in 1990 at the request of the governor. That statute and the taxpayer's revolution it subsequently engendered are discussed in Chapter 5. The New Jersey experience from *Robinson I* to the present exemplifies the fears of many state courts that entry into the thickets of school finance will inevitably lead to continual judicial oversight of the legislative-executive budgetary process and involvement in the politics of school finance and other areas of public service.

In another example, the West Virginia Supreme Court of Appeals interpreted its constitutional "thorough and efficient" clause in *Pauley v. Kelly,*[27] to require "the development of certain high quality educational standards." The court held that the ultimate goal of those high standards was to prepare "the minds, bodies and social morality" of school children "for useful and happy occupations, recreation and citizenship" and to do so "economically." The court then set forth a remarkably detailed list of specific elements of the constitutionally required educational system, holding that the system should enable each child to develop, to the best of his or her capacity, specific skills and knowledge, including literacy, computational skills, recreational pursuits, appreciation of the arts and social ethics. To facilitate the accomplishment of these goals, the court also held that the following support services were required: "(1) good physical facilities, instructional materials and personnel and (2) careful state and local supervision to prevent waste and to monitor pupil, teacher and administrative competency."

The state supreme court remanded the case to the trial court to determine whether the West Virginia system met these criteria. Implicit in its remand was the acknowledgment that the goals and principles laid down by the court were not precise enough to evaluate a school system. Rather, the supreme court said it would welcome legislative determination of standards as very important and persuasive, and to this end it required the lower court to amend the complaint to include the speaker of the house and the president of the senate as defendants. It is interesting to note that the West Virginia legislature failed to respond to this invitation to develop standards to implement the supreme court's goals and principles, and that ultimately the trial court had to appoint a special master to propose a uniform curriculum for all local school systems.[28]

Possibilities for Future Litigation

Judicial interpretation of education clauses in state constitutions may provide the best hope for reform of education systems in those states where equal protection challenges based on the state constitution have failed. It should be remembered that in *Rodriguez* the United States Supreme Court, in considering whether education was so fundamental a right that it triggered strict scrutiny analysis, asked how "education [is] to be distinguished from the significant personal interests in the basics of decent food and shelter." No doubt this conundrum weighed heavily in the consideration of the various state supreme courts. As a matter of fact, in *Robinson I*, decided several weeks after *Rodriguez,* the New Jersey Supreme Court, unlike its counterpart in California, declined to decide the issue on equal protection grounds because:

> We hesitate to turn this case upon the State equal protection clause. The reason is that the equal protection clause may be unmanageable if it is called upon to supply categorical answers in the vast area of human needs, choosing those which must be met and a single basis upon which the State must act.
>
> . . . [W]e stress how difficult it would be to find an objective basis to say the equal protection clause selects education and demands inflexible statewide uniformity in expenditure. Surely no need is more basic than food and lodging. . . . Essential also are police and fire protection, as to which the sums spent per resident vary with local decision. Nor are water and sundry public health services available throughout the State on a uniform dollar basis.[29]

Thus, *Robinson I* is the prototype case to strike down a state school financing plan solely on the basis of the state constitution's education article. The obvious attraction of this approach is to avoid constituting the judiciary a super-legislative body to allocate scarce public resources among the myriad of competing human needs. Interestingly, the supreme courts of Montana, Kentucky and Texas—at the time of writing (fall 1991), the most recent courts to hold their state's school financing law unconstitutional—did so solely on the basis of their state constitution's education clause. These cases, eschewing an equal protection argument, may prove to be a harbinger of the future (considering that the constitutions of forty-nine states have education articles). A closer look at the Texas case, *Edgewood Independent School District v. Kirby,* is instructive in this regard.

The public school financing system in Texas is similar to those in effect in most other states. Evidence indicated that spending per pupil ranged from $2,112 to $19,333; the ratio of disparity of property wealth between the richest and poorest districts was 700 to 1; and many schools could not meet state education and curriculum standards on the revenues available to them, notwithstanding a Foundation School Program designed to lessen disparities by supplementing poorer districts. The lower expenditures in the property-poor districts were not attributable to lack of tax effort. The one hundred poorest districts had an average tax rate of 74.5 cents and spent an average of $2,978 per student, while the one hundred wealthiest districts had an average tax rate of 47 cents and spent an average of $7,233 per student. Clearly, the disparities were the result of the real property wealth of the district in which the student resided.

On the basis of this evidence, the trial court concluded that the school financing system violates both the equal rights guarantee and the education clause of the Texas Constitution.[30] The trial court specifically held that education is a fundamental right, that wealth is a suspect classification in the context of school finance, that the existing funding scheme is unconstitutionally "inefficient" and that the Texas Constitution demands fiscal neutrality in public school funding. The Texas Court of Appeals reversed by a vote of 2 to 1.[31] The intermediate appellate court, relying on *Rodriguez,* held that education was not a fundamental right and wealth not a suspect classification and, thus, strict scrutiny analysis did not apply. Using traditional equal protection analysis, the court held that there was a rational relationship between local financing of school districts and the goal of local control of schools. Therefore, there was no equal protection violation. The court declined to consider the challenge under the education clause that the financing system was "inefficient," because it concluded "that which is, or is not, 'efficient' is essentially a political question not suitable for judicial review."

The Texas Supreme Court disagreed and reversed.[32] The court held "that the state's school finance system is neither financially efficient nor efficient in the sense of providing for a general diffusion of knowledge statewide" and is, therefore, unconstitutional. The court held that to constitute an efficient system:

> . . . there must be a direct and close correlation between a district's
> tax effort and the educational resources available to it; in other words,
> districts must have substantially equal access to similar revenues per
> pupil at similar levels of tax effort. Children who live in poor districts
> and children who live in rich districts must be afforded a substantial-
> ly equal opportunity to have access to educational funds. Certainly,
> this much is required if the state is to educate its populace efficient-
> ly and provide for a general diffusion of knowledge statewide.[33]

The Texas Supreme Court concluded that because it had decided that the school financing system violates the Texas Constitution's "efficiency" clause, it saw no need to consider the equal protection argument. Thus, the court avoided the necessity of determining what aspects of life are fundamental as a matter of law; yet it accomplished a significant goal of the early equal protection education reformers—it held that the money devoted to a child's education must not be a function of district wealth. This deliberate and explicit distancing of the court from overt equal protection arguments may well be the rationale which allows courts to hold school financing systems unconstitutional without, at the same time, becoming a super-legislative body setting priorities among competing human needs.

However, another avenue may exist as well under both federal and state law. Significantly, in both *Rodriguez* and *Levittown*, the respective high courts expressly noted that no evidence had been introduced to indicate that any child had not received a minimally adequate education. Plaintiffs' main contention in these cases was that some children received a lower quality education than others. This, the courts held, did not constitute denial of equal protection because it was rationally related to a legitimate state objective—local control of schools. However, these holdings leave open the possibility of a substantive due process argument that certain children are receiving an education that does not meet the minimum standards required by the state constitution or are being deprived of a minimally adequate education.

In this context, the phrase "minimally adequate" does not mean some normative universal standard of minimal adequacy; rather, it means a uniquely determined legislative or judicial standard which may be enforced by the courts. Thus, even if only one student alleges that he is not receiving that quantum of education that is constitutionally required, he may receive redress from the courts. For example, in New York a court could interpret the state constitution's requirement that the legislature provide for a system of education in a manner similar to the decisions in New Jersey and West Virginia. It could hold that the term "system" implies at least a minimally adequate system and, in the absence of legislative standards for adequacy, set forth its own. Of course, the court would probably give persuasive weight to any standards that the legislature might actually enact.

Judicial observations that no evidence of actual educational inadequacy had been introduced, much less proven, demonstrates that that argument has yet to be made in a serious and effective manner. In summary, the argument is that the state constitution requires a certain minimum level of educational quality and that the state has failed to provide that level to certain students. The actual level of education would have to be determined independently for each state, either by legislative enactment or judicial interpretation. This scenario, however remote, may ultimately provide a means to reopen closed judicial doors in New York and other states. As previously discussed in this chapter, a new lawsuit has recently been instigated in New York, alleging "gross and glaring inadequacy."[34]

The issue of federal involvement in school financing may also have remaining life. It was again referred to by the United States Supreme Court in *Papasan v. Allain* in 1986.[35] Petitioners therein challenged state funding disparities caused by unique historical circumstances in connection with school land grants in Mississippi. Although the Court rejected the conclusory allegations that they had been deprived of a minimally adequate education, it alluded to the statement in *Rodriguez* "that some identifiable quantum of education is a constitutionally protected prerequisite to the meaningful exercise of [first amendment rights]." The Supreme Court in *Papasan* further tantalized school reformers by stating that, "this Court has not yet definitively settled the questions whether a minimally adequate education is a fundamental right and whether a statute alleged to discriminatorily infringe that right should be accorded heightened equal protection review." This would appear to leave a federal door open to those who believe that a minimally adequate education is a federal constitutional right. Time will tell whether this avenue proves fruitful.

We shall now turn our attention to a consideration of the situation in New York State after the New York Court of Appeals' decision in *Levittown*. In Chapter 5, "The Current Situation: Power and Politics After Levittown," we shall analyze the political and fiscal situation in New York that has developed since 1982, when the likelihood of a high court judicial ruling against the state educational financing system was considered probable, and assess the impact that recent developments have had on the status of equality of educational opportunity in New York State. We shall also consider other developments that suggest additional possibilities for change.

NOTES

1. Ellwood P. Cubberly, *School Funds and Their Apportionment* (New York: Columbia University, Teachers College, 1905).
2. For a general discussion, see Scott Nelson," Wealth Classification and Equal Protection: Quo Vadimus?" *Houston Law Review* (1982), p. 713.
3. Arthur E. Wise, *Rich Schools, Poor Schools: The Promise of Equal Educational Opportunity* (Chicago: University of Chicago Press, 1967).
4. *McInnis v. Shapiro*, 293 F.Supp. 327 (N.D. Ill. 1968), *aff'd sub nom McInnis v. Ogilvie*, 394 U.S. 322, 89 S.Ct. 1197, 226 Ed.2d 308 (1969).
5. John E. Coons, William H. Clune and Stephen D. Sugarman, *Private Wealth and Public Education* (Cambridge: Harvard University Press, 1970).
6. See, e.g., *Plyler v. Doe*, 457 U.S. 202, 102 S.Ct. 2382, 72 L.Ed.2d 786 (1982).
7. *Serrano v. Priest*, 5 Cal. 3d 584, 96 Cal. Rptr. 601, 487 P.2d 1241 (1971) *(Serrano I)*.
8. Ibid.
9. *San Antonio Independent School Dist. v. Rodriguez*, 411 U.S. 1, 93 S.Ct. 1278, 36 L.Ed.2d 16 (1973).
10. *Serrano v. Priest*, 18 Cal. 3d 728, 135 Cal. Rptr. 345, 557 P.2 929 (1976), *cert. denied*, 432 U.S. 902 (1977) *(Serrano II)*.
11. *Board of Education, Levittown Union Free School District v. Nyquist*, 57 N.Y.2d 27, 453 N.Y.S.2d 643, 439 N.E. 2d 359 (1982), *appeal dismissed*, 459 U.S. 1139 (1983).
12. *Board of Education, Levittown Union Free School District v. Nyquist*, 94 Misc 2d 466, 408 N.Y.S. 2d 606 (1978)
13. *Board of Education, Levittown Union Free School District v. Nyquist*, 83 A.D.2d 217, 443 N.Y.S.2d 841 (1981).
14. *New York State Special Task Force on Equity and Excellence in Education*, Albany, N.Y., February 1982.
15. *Board of Education, Levittown* (1983), op. cit.
16. *Donohue v. Copiague Union Free School District*, 47 N.Y.2d 440, 418 N.Y.S.2d 375, 391 N.E.2d 1352 (1979).
17. *Board of Education, Levittown* (1983), op. cit.
18. *Reform Educational Financing Inequities Today, et al. v. Mario M. Cuomo, et al.*, Index No. 2500/1991, Nassau County Supreme Court.

19. *Robinson v. Cahill,* 70 N.J. 155, 358 A.2d 457, *inj. dissolved,* 70 N.J. 464, 360 A.2d 400 (1976) *(Robinson VI).*
20. *Brown v. Board of Education,* 347 U.S. 483, 74 S.C. 688, 98 L.Ed. 873 (1975).
21. *Baker v. Carr,* 369 U.S. 186, 82 S.C. 691, 7 L.Ed.2d 663 (1962).
22. *Robinson v. Cahill,* 62 N.J. 473, 303 A.2d 273, *cert. denied,* 414 U.S. 976 (1973) *(Robinson I).*
23. N.J. Stat. Ann. 18A:7A-4, 7A-5.
24. *Robinson v. Cahill,* 69 N.J. 449, 355, A.2d 129 (1976) *(Robinson V).*
25. *Abbott v. Burke,* 119 N.J. 287, 575 A.2d 359 (1990).
26. Ibid.
27. *Pauley v. Kelly,* 162 W. Va. 672, 255 S.E.2d 859 (1979).
28. *Pauley v. Bailey,* 324 S.E.2d 128 (1984).
29. *Robinson v. Cahill* (1973), op. cit.
30. *Edgewood Independent School District v. Kirby,* No. 362, 516, Texas 250th District Court (judgment entered June 1, 1987).
31. *Kirby v. Edgewood Independent School District,* 761 S.W.2d 859 (Tex. Ct. App. 1988)
32. *Edgewood independent School District v. Kirby,* 777 S.W.2d 391 (Tex. 1989)
33. Ibid.
34. *Reform Educational Financing Inequities Today, et al. v. Mario M. Cuomo, et al.,* Index No. 2500/1991, Nassau County Supreme Court.
35. *Papasan v. Allain,* 478 U.S. 265, 106 S. Ct. 2932, 92 L.Ed.2d 209 (1986).

5.
THE CURRENT SITUATION

The analysis shows that recent legislation to improve the equity and efficiency of the New York school finance system has not significantly reduced disparities or intercepted the link between wealth and expenditure. Adjustment in formula elements and minor programmatic initiatives cannot improve the system without a substantial rise in state funds. Both equity and efficiency are difficult to achieve without incurring costs, be they political costs of redistributive schemes such as the Regents' or the Governor's, or the dollar cost of increased support, as recommended by the Rubin Task Force. In New York State, disequalizing and equalizing elements continue to conflict within the system. The motion they produce is not like that of a pendulum; reform is not followed by counterreform. Rather the legislature continues to respond to the need for change on an ad hoc basis, creating a school finance system that is inconsistent, "schizophrenic," and increasingly complex.

> —Joan Scheuer, "The Equity of New York
> State's System of Financing Schools"

Political and Fiscal Developments
After *Levittown*

"We no longer have a court-pointed gun to our head," exclaimed Assemblyman Leonard Stavisky, on hearing of the June 1982 decision of the New York Court of Appeals to overrule the rulings of the two lower courts in *Levittown v. Nyquist*.[1] The immediate reaction to the

Levittown decision was generally one of relief on the part of political leaders, especially those in the legislature. A possible constitutional crisis had been averted and the stability of the system had been assured through the avoidance of fractious changes that would have been mandated by a court ruling against the state. All sides to the dispute affirmed their commitment to the hallowed goals of equality: the plaintiffs in a mood of disappointment and resentment and the leading state political figures with assertions of conciliation and hope for resolution and progress through normal political channels.

When Leonard Stavisky, then chairman of the Assembly Education Committee, made the comment about the "court-pointed gun," he implied that the onus was now on the legislature to demonstrate good faith and commitment to the goals of equality. The conviction was expressed even more clearly by then Governor Hugh Carey when he stated: "It's not for me to quarrel with the court's findings. I still hold with the philosophy that it is the function of the state under the Regents to equalize educational opportunity for the residents of our state."[2]

For years, legislative leaders had been asserting that educational finance was their prerogative and that the court should not meddle, but instead leave it to the legislature itself to develop a remedy. Now that the judicial decision had essentially complied with that wish, attention was focused upon the legislature with the political hot-foot of equality now in its court.

The state's highest court, the New York Court of Appeals, held that the existing system of educational finance was constitutional. But it also acknowledged the existence of many undesirable characteristics, especially the range of disparities in per-pupil expenditures, a holding similar to that of the United States Supreme Court in *Rodriguez v. San Antonio Independent School District.* However, it charged the legislature with the responsibility for remedying these faults, asserting that the "primary responsibility for the provision of fair and equitable educational opportunity within the financial capabilities of our state's taxpayers unquestionably rests with that branch of government."[3]

It is instructive to depict how the political system responded to that ruling. Essentially, the familiar elements of the budgetary charade have continued to dominate events during these years. All parties asserted their support of the goals of equity and equality, and this time in an even more grandiose manner, as befitted the politics of the post-*Levittown* era. A newly elected governor pronounced a strong commitment to principles of equality, advocating the elimination of save-harmless proposals and special attention to the needs of poor districts. Legislative leaders, more responsive to the needs of their majorities, and therefore more cautious, joined in endorsing the goals of equity and equality, but refrained from supporting any proposal that would reduce the amount of aid currently being received by school districts, contemptuously dismissing this as the "Robin Hood" approach to the pursuit of equality.

As budget approval deadlines drew near, many revisions and compromises were negotiated, but the essential and determining elements of the process remained the same. The protection of the shares of all members' districts took precedence over significant movement toward equality. While economic and fiscal factors might dictate the size of the pie—the aggregate amount of additional state aid that would be made available—politics would determine the size of the slice that each district would receive.

Ideals and goals of equity and equality, while good stuff for public pronouncements, are in reality often mere rhetoric to be used in the process of accommodation necessary to the forging of each majority conference consensus required for budget approval. The response to initial proposals for equality that would result in losses for individual districts is aptly reflected in the reaction of one lobbyist, representing more affluent school districts, to Governor Mario Cuomo's most recent "Robin Hood" budget proposals that called for a significant shift of aid from wealthy to poor school districts. Agreeing that the only bright spot in these proposals was the dim chance of approval by the legislature, the lobbyist counseled, "Tell the folks back home it's just another computer printout."[4] This reflects the understanding of veterans seasoned in the annual budgetary process who make a shrewd distinction between necessary forms of political posturing and the actual outcomes that will result.

The political lineup each year followed traditional patterns. The New York State Board of Regents established its position in the vanguard of equality advocates calling for the elimination of all save-harmless and flat grant provisions, while at the same time seeking to tie state aid to local tax effort. The Regents usually call for an increase in local tax effort and a significant reduction in the amount of state aid given to wealthier districts. It is this latter proposal that annually relegates the regents' package to the land of political "no-nos," since no legislature attuned to political reality would seriously entertain such a resolution.

The New York State Educational Conference Board, representing a diversity of mainline powerful education interest groups, will usually call for a larger package of aid in the aggregate but with not as much tampering with save-harmless provisions or emphasis on equality. The governor then makes his initial budget submissions by staking out the high ground of equality, but also limiting recommended increases in state aid to a sum significantly less than that of the Regents or conference board. The legislature, taking its cue from its leadership as to the aggregate sum that will be available for state aid, first agrees on the division between New York City and the rest of the state, and then proceeds to divide the aid in a manner that will satisfy interests in the party conference in each house. This time-honored scenario has long dictated the outcomes of educational finance and continues into the post-*Levittown* era of school finance.

The recommendations of the New York State Special Task Force on Equity and Excellence in Education (the Rubin Task Force), were an unusual and important contribution to the political debate in 1982. This commission was created as a special task force in September 1978 in response to the ruling of Justice L. Kingsley Smith in the *Levittown* case declaring the educational finance system of New York State to be unconstitutional. The task force was charged by then Governor Carey with the responsibility for devising constructive state responses to the possibilities of a court ruling that would overturn the state system of educational finance. Unlike its predecessor, the Fleischmann Commission, which had recommended radical reform with the complete state assumption of financing responsibilities, the Rubin Task Force responded to its mandate cautiously, anxious not to violate or trespass the boundaries of legislative toleration.

The work was conducted during a three-year period, with its final report submitted in February of 1982.[5] A variety of proposals were developed that provided alternative approaches to the equity issue, essentially leaving it to the legislature to act in favor of more or less equalization. This involved choices among the different total costs assigned to each package, which resulted from tinkering with such mainstays of the education finance system as the percentage equalizing formula, definitions of wealth and pupil counts, adaptations of the aid formula to include attention to special needs, overburdens and cost of living variations. The extra cost to the state of these recommendations ranged from $500 million to $1.5 billion, the higher sum representing significantly greater progress toward equality. Although much of the impetus for the task force was diluted as a result of the decision of the New York Court of Appeals, the Rubin Commission has had an important influence on the education proposals of both Governors Carey and Cuomo.

Budgetary Outcomes and the Impact on Equalization

At the request of Assembly Speaker Stanley Fink, the New York Assembly Committees on Education and Ways and Means held a series of ten regional joint hearings in the fall of 1983 for the purpose of making a "bottom-to-top re-evaluation of New York State's system of providing and financing quality education."[6] Testimony was taken from civic and community leaders and educational professionals across the state who represented a cross-section of educational interests. The committee published a special report summarizing the hearings which included the submission of a five-year educational reform plan, entitled "Setting Priorities for New York State."[7]

Special attention was given to equal opportunity as the most "intractable problem involving the wide spending disparities among schools which directly result in highly unequal educational opportunities for many school children across the state." The report stated that "although the average expenditure during the 1982-83 school year was $4,302 per pupil in New York State, the highest amount in the lower 48 states, some low wealth school districts spent only $2,350 per pupil, a little more than half the state average for all school districts."

As a result of the decision to focus on education, coordinated with the assembly strategy to dramatize this concern by holding special hearings, the legislature enacted what was then the largest single increase in state education aid in history—$499 million. However, the price of passage, as usual, required the elimination of many of the more equalizing proposals contained in earlier aid proposals, especially that of the governor which called for the elimination of save-harmless and basic flat grant provisions. The need to be responsive to pressures for greater equality is reflected in the assertion of the Assembly Education Committee's report that among its accomplishments for the year was "reforming the operating aid formula to make it more equitable by giving equal weight to income and real property and enriching it by $241.79 million."

Policy pronouncements and posturing aside, "let's look at the record," as Al Smith once said. The record we choose to examine covers the school years since 1982, the date of the *Levittown* decision. Since this period involved the highest absolute sums of increased aid ever, the expectation is that lessening of disparities would be more likely to occur at this time.

Table 7 depicts the distribution of state aid, starting with school year 1979-80 and leading up to 1989-90. This portrays the last three years of the pre-*Levittown* era and the years subsequent to the New York Court of Appeals' decision, when the legislature was once more acknowledged as being the main arbiter of laws affecting school finance. As a result of a new commitment to increase funding to education, state aid rose dramatically, both in terms of absolute size and percentages. Aid increased at a size and rate unparalleled in legislative history, surprising professional observers who annually anticipated curtailment of this trend.

State aid to education was clearly established as the prime issue of legislative concern. But it is very doubtful that such levels of increase in aid can be replicated any time in the near future in view of the impact of the current fiscal crisis. This is likely to lead to even greater conflict between proponents of increased school aid and advocates of equity. Only this time, the argument will be over the allocation of smaller sums of state aid.

The previous great success in expanding the flow of state educational aid can be attributed to a number of factors: the vastly improved economic situation of the state; the commitment by the state to an expanded role as a response to the *Levittown* suit; the importance of the Rubin Commission recommendations in building a consensus for change; and the pressure brought by various educational interest groups, who were now joined into a more effective coalition for increasing state aid. Of special importance was the role played by political leaders committed to enhancing the state role in education. We have already mentioned Speaker of the Assembly Stanley Fink, who took the lead in this struggle by creating a special task force, the recommendations of which served as guidelines for legislative action. John Curley describes the process in the following manner:

> The State commitment to provide substantially increased financial support for education illustrates the role a single, powerful, state-level actor can have in determining public policy. Colella and Beam have termed such individuals a public entrepeneur or someone who assumes responsibility and becomes the chief advocate for a project, program or policy. In New York, the Speaker of the Assembly and second most powerful Democrat in State government after the Governor, appears to have filled this role by establishing a political framework which helped spawn the large increases in State aid to schools.[8]

Fink and others took the lead because of their commitment to a more active state role in education as well as a sense of outrage regarding the injustices against poor districts that were referred to by plaintiffs in the *Levittown* suit. However, political pressures for a greater state role developed from two sources: those representing the interests of poorer areas who wanted more attention to their needs and those educational interest groups who sought more state aid across the board in order to improve the quality of the educational system.

Being seasoned and practical-minded legislators, Fink and others understood the limits to legislative action for radical reform. Thus, they aggressively sought to expand overall state aid, yet avoid emphasis on equity issues that might undermine the political coalition required to achieve more state aid. They were able to succeed in increasing total funds for education. As to the reduction of disparities, however, our findings are somewhat different.

As per-pupil expenditure disparities between poorer and wealthier districts increased, overall state aid rose significantly. This is reflected in both Table 4 and Chart 2, which portray the expenditure gap between the 10th and 90th percentile districts in both absolute and proportional terms. The difference between the 10th and the 90th percentile increased steadily both before and after the *Levittown* decision. In fact, resistance to equalization after *Levittown* was what mobilized many of the save-harmless districts to pressure for the creation and expansion of supplemental and high tax aids in order to protect their share of state aid.

There remains a strong correlation between district property and income wealth and expenditures per pupil. Local wealth values per pupil remain the single most important factor determining the level of educational expenditures, not state aid or local tax effort. And this even at a time when large increases might have been expected to have at least some effect on disparities. The increasing gap is primarily due to the ability of wealthier districts to increase their tax rates. However, the gap also reflects the fact that the state aid formula has not been successful in equalizing the disparities. The gap continues to increase in spite of the fact that the aid package has become much larger.

Analysis of the components of state aid also helps in understanding its limiting impact as regards equalization. While total state aid showed a large increase, aid programs not included in the state aid formula— which usually do not have an equalizing intent—showed larger proportional increases. Significant increases were made in various categorical programs and "other" forms of operating aid, thereby assuring that an even larger proportion of the aid would go to less needy districts. The operating-aid portion of state aid, which has the greatest equalizing impact because its distribution is inversely related to local property wealth, rose at a lesser rate than did the other programs. Save-harmless and basic flat grants were retained, thereby assuring that no district would receive less aid than in the previous year. The introduction and continued expansion of new aids, such as supplementary school and high tax aid, were additional devices developed for the purpose of undermining the equalizing intent of the operating aid formula.

The experiences of the last few years provide a good benchmark with which to assess the possibilities for reduction of disparities. The amount of state aid increased to levels not expected and not likely to be soon duplicated, yet inequalities as measured by absolute or proportional differences actually increased. The large increase in the size of the pie meant an increase in the size of each slice, but the differences among those at the table grew larger. The legislature was better able to rise to the challenge of raising more revenue than it was to deal with conflicts involved in redistribution. What this augurs for succeeding years, a time when such plentiful sources of new aid will probably not be available, and may in fact actually decline, is a subject which we shall consider at the end of this chapter.

The Retreat from Equality

Efforts by states to equalize the financial resources of school districts, a major goal of educational reformers in the 1970's, have not significantly reduced the gap between the richest and poorest districts, according to school finance experts.

In some states, the experts say, the disparities of wealth and spending have increased. Efforts to equalize spending have fallen short, they say, partly because poorer districts have not been able to muster the political power necessary to channel the bulk of increased state aid their way and partly because an emphasis on equalizing finances has shifted to an emphasis on improving educational standards.

"I don't see the reforms of the 1970's holding up," said G. Alan Hickrod, president of the American Finance Association, which is made up of school financial officers, academics and educational consultants. "We've lost almost all the ground we had gained."[9]

As a result of the decision of the New York Court of Appeals in

Levittown in June 1982, attention was once more directed to the legislative and political process as the central determinant of educational expenditures. The court ruling in 1982 marked the end of an era in the struggle for equality in New York, since it apparently closed off the last option for significant change that had activated the educational reform movement during the 1960s. The long drawn-out process of the *Levittown* case nurtured the hope for major change. Because, from its initial inception in the trial court, the case lasted nine years and because the state's position was rejected by two pro-reform rulings in the trial and intermediate appellate courts, many reformers believed that at last the goal of equality would be achieved.

One by one, all the promising possibilities that had encouraged change in the 1960s have been thwarted. The expectations had been that although judicial activism could represent an immediate triumph, other factors were bound to lead to victory, even if at a somewhat slower pace. The climate of opinion indicated strong public support for increased governmental activism for redistribution and compensatory policies. Optimism regarding the economy reinforced belief that this would be made politically palatable by high rates of growth, and intense political activism lent credence to optimism that change would occur. Now the situation has dramatically changed, and there is little hope regarding any of these possibilities.

For some time, the climate of opinion in the nation had been shifting toward the right, but there was uncertainty as to how durable this trend would be. First signs had occurred in the late 1960s with the election of Richard Nixon, but the Watergate fiasco stayed the shifting political tides, a delay that only served to broaden and intensify the nature of the conservative transformation—an event more clearly signified by the election of Ronald Reagan in 1980. Regarding social programs, the new and dominant view was clear. The main domestic goal of the new administration was to stimulate economic growth by tax decreases along with large increases in military expenditures. These changes were initiated under traditional conservative banners and slogans of the goal of a balanced budget. This meant that many domestic programs were either targets for restrictions and cuts or were at best considered as a burden to be tolerated while pursuing the main goals of the new government: economic growth and the expansion of the military sectors.

In this redefinition of purpose and policy, there remained little room for expanding visions of social policy or even for the maintenance of past efforts. Education especially was vulnerable, inasmuch as it was more easily relegated to the role of a traditional state and local function. Compensatory educational programs of the Great Society were rejected as representing a meddlesome and ineffectual intrusion of the federal government into local affairs.[10]

All educational programs were subject to intense scrutiny and often severely cut. This had a special impact on those federal compensatory programs oriented to the needs of disadvantaged children. Fiscal Year 1985 outlays for such programs dropped 20 percent below the pre-Reagan period in real terms.[11] This does not take into account additional significant budget cuts that have been proposed for subsequent years. Federal monies for local school districts were also reduced because of these cuts. Federal aid, which had risen in 1979-80 to 5.4 percent of total educational expenditures for elementary and secondary education in New York State, dropped to 3.1 percent in 1988-89. (See Table 2.)[12] The hopes that once existed for significant federal aid directed toward goals of equality and equity were now shattered. It was clear that the sails of expanding federal social policy were being drawn in and hopes for greater equity would have to be met, if at all, at the local and state levels.

But the basic underpinning of reliance and faith in an increased federal role had already been marred by other developments. The vision of the Great Society was painless progress based upon trickle-down economics. This asserted that if the Gross National Product was made larger in the aggregate, all groups in the society would benefit, thereby avoiding painful choices relating to distribution and fairness. This optimism flowed from a confidence that finally the business cycle had been tamed and new techniques of macroeconomic planning enabled government to fine-tune and manipulate the economy so as to achieve desirable levels of growth. This optimism was also buttressed by the belief that the nation was rich and powerful enough to afford both guns and butter without shifting to a high-tax/low-consumption war economy during the Vietnam period.

The confidence of that period was shattered by successive developments of unparalleled rates of post-World War II inflation and recession that rudely brought home the fact that there were untamed elements remaining in the economy. These developments undermined the faith in continued economic growth and in the power of the federal government to manage the economy. The perception that the pie was in fact not growing but decreasing led to increased opposition to taxes and pressure for less interventionist governmental policies, especially regarding social programs for poor people.

The collapse of faith in the federal role was bound to have an important effect on local and state planning for education. Although federal aid in total never amounted at its peak to more than 10 percent of total expenditures for public elementary and secondary schools (see Table 1), its importance was considerably greater. To the extent that the federal government has been the most equity-oriented in its policies, it set a standard against which localities were judged. It also provided leadership and a moral tone that set a higher standard of equity that could be imposed as a requirement for receiving aid. It further was involved in the development of equity measures that would serve as standards for assessing the performance of educational finance systems in the fifty states.

It had always been a truism of American politics that fiscal support of equity was more likely, the more distant and removed government was from local considerations and pressures. Although the history of educational finance in this country indicates that state governments play the major role, the federal government was seen as the new super-equalizer, a situation made possible by its access to far more plentiful sources of revenue and also by its relative insulation from local interests and pressures. Now, educational reformers confronted a situation where that hope was fading, and this at the very time that the New York Court of Appeals was deciding against attempts to reform the system in New York through judicial intervention.

A last but extremely important factor must be considered in assessing the changing equation of forces pressing for equality. Policy making in the 1960s was greatly influenced by the perception that social stability was threatened because of the large numbers of poor and minority persons who were disaffected from the political system. The fact that poor people functioned as an active force at the local level was a threat to the stability of the political system. The politics of protest and riots had captured the attention of policy makers, compelling some form of response, and that response usually took the form of social programs of some kind, often involving education.

Now that the economy had tightened and political orientations shifted, there was a declining receptivity to the calls for reform and attention to social needs. As the larger society was more resistant and less attentive, it seemed also that there was less energy and passion for change on the part of the aggrieved minority. Regarding the nexus of relationships between these dynamics, we shall not speculate; it seems clear that is what occurred. And the result was to remove a major force that had been responsible for the expansion of social programs under the Great Society. At the same time, it was more than likely that this new set of attitudes and developments could not fail to have an impact on the way in which business was conducted at the state and local level and on the state of educational inequalities—which is, after all, the main focus of our analysis.

Possibilities for Change

A long-term aspiration of educational reformers in New York State has been the fashioning of a coalition of those school districts that would gain from a reduction of inequalities. But a major obstacle to such a coalition has been the disparate nature of other interests and goals existing among potential participants. The state consists of a variety of political cultures that defy grouping along traditional lines of class or ideology. The upstate-downstate split has always reflected intense rural and big city divisions, originally related to the disadvantaged position of poor rural areas as contrasted with the wealthier big cities of the nineteenth and early twentieth centuries. The dominance of New York City added a special character to these classic distinctions, since its immense wealth and power gave it a status unique and apart from traditional rural-urban dichotomies. In fact, the large upstate cities tended to identify with their rural hinterland rather than with the interests of a downstate big city, which is often associated negatively with a different political and ethnic culture.

Much of New York State politics before the United States Supreme Court's landmark reapportionment decision in *Baker v. Carr* consisted of a state legislature dominated and controlled by rural interests, diverting the wealth of New York City to other areas of the state. Expectations at the time were that reapportionment would, by assuring equal representation, result in greater political power for large cities. However, reapportionment, coming as it did at a time of great outward migration of population from central cities to suburbs, resulted in the lack of an independent majority for city, suburban or rural interests. This brought about the creation of a natural alliance, based on historical, political and social value affinities, among suburbs, upstate rural and smaller urban areas. This alliance forms the basis of a majority coalition in the New York State Senate and also serves as a limiting factor to the reach of the Democratic majority in the New York State Assembly, since it has the power to outweigh and override the interests of New York City and the other large central cities.

The possibilities of developing a single issue coalition for educational reform and equalization, which would bring together members representing districts with low wealth who would seek aid formulas having greater equalization, has always seemed a chimeric vision due to the perception that there existed no commonality of interest that cut across traditional splits in the political culture of of New York State. It was generally assumed that legislative districting resulted in the creation of individual member seats with diverse school district constituencies, both poor and wealthy, and with different and conflicting interests and values regarding the disbursement of state aid. Hence, the legislator, in responding to the interests of this diverse constituency, would express a conservative, status quo oriented position. The goal would be to achieve as much aid as possible for all school districts within a legislator's province, especially the larger constituency blocks, and at the least to assure that no school district would be reduced.

For the first time, as a result of advances in computer mapping techniques and the efforts of the Legislative Task Force on Reapportionment and Demographics, we now have available a breakdown by population as to how each school district is distributed within a senate and assembly district. Table 10 presents data that refute many of the assumptions about the school district representation of legislative districts and helps us to understand the source of educational finance pressures that are brought to bear on each legislator. The data indicate that a potential exists for forming a coalition for educational reform in the assembly by putting together New York City representatives and other Democratic legislators who represent areas that consist primarily of property-poor school districts.

At the current time (1991), the Democratic majority in the assembly consists of ninety-five members with fifty-seven representing districts from New York City. The combination of New York City together with some of the thirty-eight from other areas in the state could be enough to form a coalition for educational reform. The senate Republican majority of thirty-five consists of seven New York City members as well as some other representatives with significant upstate big city and rural constituencies who would be sympathetic to the interests of the assembly majority. Such a coalition might be able to develop a strong bargaining position in negotiations with the senate.

However, the distinctly different problems that confront upstate and downstate areas militate against the formation of such a coalition. In addition, the intensity of involvement in educational finance differs greatly among those representing the dependent school districts in the Big Five cities and those who represent independent school districts.

Especially within New York City, there is often greater concern with the dimensions of non-educational portions of the state budget which are related to inner-city needs than there is with education itself.

The reason why it is doubtful that a strong coalition around equal educational opportunity can be developed is because most legislators represent both wealthy and poor school districts. This leads to an inclination toward stability-oriented, status quo politics that protect the level of existing shares of aid. Also, many members, especially those from New York City and the other four large cities, have little interest in the aid formula since they represent areas with dependent school districts. In addition, the traditional animosity toward New York City undermines efforts to develop a broad-based coalition around a single issue, such as educational aid, even though the number of potential beneficiaries might provide the basis of a legislative majority.

In Chapters 1 and 4, we have paid attention to the manner in which educational reformers, disappointed with past attempts at achieving change through the courts, have developed a new concept of minimal educational adequacy with which to assert that certain individual students are receiving a substandard education. This type of challenge was not foreclosed by either the United States Supreme Court in *Rodriguez* or the New York Court of Appeals in *Levittown,* and was in concept upheld in both the *Robinson* and *Pauley* cases in New Jersey and West Virginia respectively. It is difficult to forecast the success that this approach is likely to encounter in New York since under this concept each state sets its own standards of education, either legislatively or, by default, judicially. Nevertheless, the possibility exists that there will be an increase in such challenges in the future, especially in those states where the equal protection argument has been rejected by the courts.

We have discussed in Chapter 3 how the key element allocating state aid between New York City and the rest of the state is agreed upon through prior determination of the leaders. The importance of the New York City division is critical to an understanding of how the aid formula operates and why it is that the equalizing impact of the aid formula is limited. Essentially it is the level of New York City aid that determines how the formula will affect the other seven hundred twenty-four school districts. Members and staff cannot proceed on any details of the aid package until the leadership has agreed on the New York City slice of the pie. Only after that agreement has been reached is it possible to determine how much money will be available and how the aid package will be constructed for the other seven hundred twenty-four districts.

The remaining portion of aid is then allocated to achieve the necessary political goals of protecting all districts, assuring that none will receive less aid than it did the previous year. It is at this stage that the save-harmless and basic flat grant features become important in driving the formula to implement that goal. Success in reducing disparities is limited because of the fact that New York City's large share of total aid is not driven by the formula, but is in fact determined by pre-agreement of the leaders.

The major goal of the legislature is to hammer out an agreement that will secure support of the majority in each house. This cannot be done unless a basic condition is met, the satisfaction of member interests. The prime interest is assurance that at the minimum a district will not have its aid reduced below the level of the previous year. Regardless of how the formula might be changed in a technical manner to produce more equality, the political process at work in the legislature will superimpose its own determining political needs and interests over the intended purposes of the formula.

The more than half-century focus of educational reformers upon revision and manipulation of the aid formula to achieve goals of greater equality have been regularly subverted by the subordination of the formula to legislative purposes. The concentration of reformers upon formula changes has resulted from a distorted perspective as to where the appropriate levers for change exist. Because of this, attention has been diverted from the need for the structural change in the legislative decision-making process that must be implemented before equalization can occur.

What we are asserting in the last analysis is that it is the political process and political forces that really determine equity in school aid and not quasi-scientific formulas developed by staff and technicians. We have described the situation in detail as it functions in New York State. This is substantially repeated throughout the nation. The tragic consequence of this system is the failure of American society to provide an equal educational opportunity for all students, a failure which is due to the political nature of the legislative decision-making process. We cannot expect a legislative body to divest itself of such political behavior. It is the "nature of the beast" that legislative decision making is political. However, since this condition is growing worse, and disparities are likely to increase even more, some action must be taken to remedy this situation.

Politics cannot and should not be taken out of the legislative process. Therefore, consideration must be given to removing the state aid allocation process from control of the legislature. This could be done by turning the allocation process over to an "expert" non-political body. Generically, what comes to mind in this context are educational oversight agencies, e.g., in New York, the New York State Board of Regents. Typically, such agencies have been in the forefront of advocating increased school equality.

We must emphasize that we are not suggesting that these non-legislative bodies determine the size of the education budget. This is and must remain a legislative function. The legislature should make the determination as to the percent of total state revenues which are to be made available in each year for educational purposes. The expert body would then decide upon the allocation of this sum of money to the various school districts.

While on the surface it might appear that the legislature would resist such changes, there are indications that this need not be the case. Given the unlikely possibility of maintaining the current level of state aid increases in the future, it is expected that there will be increasingly intense competition for limited funds. Distributing this limited pie will become an increasingly difficult political burden. Moving the function of specific allocation to an independent neutral education agency will remove the legislature from the political hot seat and reduce the intense pressures that are regularly brought to bear on legislators. At the same time, retaining the power to determine the aggregate sums and shares going to education will preserve their preeminent political status.

Of course, in most cases a legislative body would not act to remove itself from the allocation process. Therefore, the only realistic manner in which this goal could be attained would be through the route of constitutional amendment. This type of approach has already been followed in several states in another subject area. We have experienced the constitutional creation of non-partisan independent commissions to reapportion state legislatures where the political process has rendered the legislature of the state impotent to deal with the requirements of law and justice. We advocate the same approach to the irresolvable difficulties of educational finance.

In those states where the legislature must originate the constitutional amendment process, it would be very rare for a legislative body to take the first step to dilute its power. Therefore, realistically, we would expect as disparities widen and equality lessens that the results of that condition will become more troublesome. Those states that allow the constitutional amendment process to be commenced through intitiative of the people would then take the lead in attempting to remove educational aid formulas from the political process and repose them in neutral, non-political bodies.

We are aware that this may be considered an elitist and anti-democratic approach to the extent that power is being taken from the people's representatives, the legislature. However, American state legislatures have clearly failed to provide an equal educational opportunity for school children, one of their most important functions in the polity, and consequently there must be some redress. We suggest this as a pragmatic adaptation to a particular situation rather than as a general criticism of the failing of the legislative and political process.

Our proposal to develop an independent body to preside over the distribution of state aid is essentially an intermediate step of reform that would not result in full fiscal equalization. Local districts would still be able to raise as much monies as they wish to and this would result in significant inequalities. The only way in which inequalities related to differences in local wealth could be fully eliminated would be through state assumption of full funding of public elementary and secondary education. In that way, all differences in expenditures per pupil would reflect a determination based upon educational need rather than local wealth differences. Of course, as we further dicuss in Chapter 6, there are many political difficulties that undermine the possibility of such a proposal being adopted. However, we make mention of full state funding because it represents the extreme range on the continuum of posssibilites for reform. It also presents an alternative that might make some of the other possiblities we have discussed more acceptable as compromise measures.

The Perennial Issue of School Finance

There has been a recent surge of interest in our subject, additional evidence of its durability. A convergence of events—economic, political and judicial—makes the current period an especially exciting time for issues related to educational finance.

The 1980s were witness to a great expansion in state aid for local elementary and secondary schools. This resulted in the expectation that there would be regular increases in state educational aid. The current national economic recession, especially impacting the Northeast, has placed severe pressures on many states to not only reduce the rate of increase, but to mandate significant absolute reductions in some states.

For example, Governor Mario Cuomo of New York announced the existence of a $6 billion budget gap in 1991 and proposed a reduction of $900 million in state education aid (about 10 percent of the previous year's $9 billion sum). He also proposed that the reductions be made in relationship to local district wealth, with the wealthier districts bearing the major portion of the cuts and the poorer districts being spared that burden. This is essentially a version of the "Robin Hood" in reverse with a leveling down occurring through reductions—a change from the situation of previous years, where the battle was over the distribution of shares of the annual state increase.

State education aid was a major reason for delayed approval of the total budget. Since there are no judicial mandates that determine the outcomes in New York, as in the current conflicts in New Jersey and Texas, the governor's proposals were rejected. This is because the Republican-controlled senate will not participate in any agreement that has such a negative impact on its constituency. Instead, an across-the-board reduction was enacted, resulting in an increase in inequality among school districts.

Another new development in New York State, previously discussed in Chapter 4, is the challenge to the New York State educational finance system brought by twenty poorer Long Island school districts. Recent court decisions in New Jersey, Texas and elsewhere may portend the possibilities of more positive judicial responses to challenges of state education finance systems. In that case, it may be that this latest challenge will have a different outcome than occurred in the *Levittown* case, thereby dramatically altering the situation in New York. However, we are now only entering the beginning of the long process during which this issue once more winds itself through the judicial system.

The legal situation in Texas and New Jersey is analyzed in Chapter 4, describing how the supreme courts of both states ruled that their systems of educational finance were unconstitutional under the education clause of their state constitutions. This direction of the court is an important development, opening up further possibilities for rulings favorable to equalization in a number of additional states. In both instances, the courts ordered an increase and redistribution of state aid with a capping and leveling down of the wealthier districts, resulting in the significant reduction of inequalities among the poorer districts.

In Texas, the court decision resulted in great conflict as the legislature struggled unsuccessfully on four different occasions to pass legislation that would be compatible with the decision of the Texas Supreme Court. The new law divides the state into one hundred eighty-eight special education regions, somewhat similar to county lines, and requires that within each region the wealthier districts share some of their wealth with the poorer ones.[13] It is estimated that this would cost about $1.2

billion over the next two years, with local school districts required to increase property taxes by $400 million a year. It is anticipated that most of this new money would be raised by the wealthier districts. This proposal would also dictate minimum levels of taxing and spending for all of the state's 1,047 school districts, in addition to capping the amount the most affluent districts can spend.

In New Jersey, the situation was even more difficult and conflict-ridden. In anticipation that the New Jersey State Supreme Court would strike down the state educational finance system, Governor James Florio moved to anticipate the court's decision by sponsoring the Quality Education Act of 1990.[14] This act provided for all districts to receive more total aid than originally anticipated, for the foundation level and state aid to increase and for a variety of other enhancements in different types of categorical aid. The new law would have made available an extra $1.1 billion in state aid during the 1991-92 school year. In addition to proposing a 30 percent increase in state aid, state aid would have been concentrated in low and moderate wealth areas, thereby complying with the dictate of "a thorough and efficient education," as required by the state constitution.

Subsequently, in June 1990, the New Jersey Supreme Court in *Abbott v. Burke* declared that the New Jersey educational finance system was unconstitutional in its application.[15] The court specifically called for the elimination of minimum aid, analagous to the save-harmless provisions in the New York State law, and required that the legislature raise the expenditure level of the poorest districts to substantially that of the wealthiest suburban districts, without recourse to the property wealth of the poorest districts.

Governor Florio's Quality Education Act of 1990 immediately came under great attack from those who felt they would lose out, including teachers unions, wealthier school districts and legislative leaders. They asserted that the results would be higher taxes and lower quality of education for the wealthier but with no guarantee of gains in performance for the poorer schools. This resulted in a great loss in the governor's popularity and harm to Democratic candidates in the November 1990 elections. The governor claimed he was simply seeking to fulfill the intent of the court's decision. In the minds of the voters, however, he was identified with pursuing a high tax policy to support goals of equity and equality. As statewide opposition grew and with increased fear for the survival of Democratic candidates in the 1991 legislative elections, the Democratic leadership sought changes in the Quality Education Act to lessen the political disaffection.

Finally after more than four months of dickering[16] the governor and the legislature agreed to a compromise measure that would shift $360 million from school aid to property tax relief and, in addition, place tighter limits on school spending, delay the timing of local assumption of current state payments of pension costs and eliminate provisions of the earlier bill that would have required local school tax increases in order to receive additional new state aid. Essentially, the new law provided some property tax relief, while still preserving more money for schools. However, this achievement is unlikely to satisfy those who seek the elimination of funding inequalities between rich and poor children. Since the revised law weakens progress toward that goal, a new challenge is now under way, calling for the court to strike it down for not meeting the requirements of the *Abbott* decision.

The Florio education aid proposal in New Jersey is a good demonstration of the political perils of redistribution, confirming our analysis in Chapter 3 of the political limits to equalization in New York State. The New Jersey Supreme Court ruled that the existing system must be fixed and, with that as its mandate, the administration created a package that alienated many key interests. In addition, the budgetary plan was undermined by the accompanying recession, which greatly reduced the revenues available to implement the proposal. A decline in the necessary resources, combined with the angry reactions to tax increases and aid redistribution, forced the governor to eventually accept a package which, while still somewhat equalizing, has been reduced significantly from the original proposal.

The Democratic majority in both houses was not able to survive the 1991 legislative elections and it seems unlikely that the governor will be re-elected in 1993. The issue is still being fought bitterly among the governor, local school districts, the professional educational establishment, the legislative and executive branches and soon, once again, the court. We are again witnesses to the intense nature of this issue, a continuing focus of struggle and conflict.

In comparing the Texas and New Jersey situations, we must point out that it is too early to interpret Texas in light of the agreement just passed by that state legislature. The full response of voter reaction has not yet been felt and, in many ways, Texas is now at the point where New Jersey was in June 1990 when the Quality of Education Act was passed. It may well be that voter opposition will force yet another compromise that will dilute the equalizing thrust of the new Texas law.

The experience of New Jersey demonstrates how vulnerable is the thrust for equalization when a myriad of more privileged districts and a myriad of other interests combine to oppose cuts in their aid. Also, it is especially difficult to implement redistribution policies at a time of economic recession when the conflict has shifted from increases in shares of a larger state aid package to fights over a smaller package.

Events of a different nature in recent years have placed education at the center of public attention. A *national* plan has been proposed by President Bush which calls for more "choice" opportunities among schools, providing a variety of public, private and parochial alternatives.[17] While the president's plan is only the opening salvo in the continuing debate about national direction, it is important to note its relevance to the topic at hand. He has called for changes in curriculum, school organization and educational goals. Rejecting money as being of importance in the determination of educational outcomes, he has proposed very little additional funds to respond to these new challenges. The idea of the federal government playing a role in reducing inequality is nowhere to be found in the presidential plan.

The 1990 Florio experience in New Jersey illustrates why it is that any significant movement toward fiscal equality is so very difficult. In addition, on the national level, the "Reagan revolution" has radically altered the shape of national policy and greatly diminished the possibilities for federal aid for equity-oriented policies. The lack of strong political support for equalization portends a bleak outlook for future gains through political and legislative channels.

In the next and concluding chapter, we shall consider why it is that the ideal of equality conflicts with different aspects of American society and how this undermines progress toward expanding educational opportunity.

NOTES

1. "Top State Court Upholds School Financing Basis," *New York Times*, Editorial, June 24, 1982.
2. Ibid.
3. *Levittown v. Nyquist*, 57 N.Y. 2d 27 (1982).
4. Statement by George Gerber, a lobbyist representing school boards in Westchester, Putnam and Rockland Counties, as reported in "School Aid Plan Called Devastating: Cuomo's Budget to Cut Funds for Most Districts," Gannet Newspapers, January 23, 1985.
5. *The Report and Recommendations of the New York State Special Task Force on Equity and Excellence in Education*, Albany, N.Y., February 1982.
6. New York State Assembly Committee on Education, *1984 Annual Report* (Albany: The Assembly, 1984), p. 1.
7. "Report to the Speaker on Setting Priorities for New York State Public Education; Findings and Recommendations," Assembly of the State of New York, December 28, 1983, mimeo.
8. John R. Curley, "The Relationship of Education Advocacy to State Aid for Schools in New York," *Journal of Education Finance* 12, No. 2 (Fall 1986), p. 228.
9. Jonathan Friendly, "The Disparity in Resources," *New York Times*, January 9, 1985, p. B1.
10. In fact, not only were they considered ineffectual, but according to a new and influential critique, it was charged that these programs actually caused a deterioration in the very conditions they were devised to remedy. For a presentation of these views, see, Charles Murray, *Losing Ground: American Social Policy 1950-1980* (New York: Basic Books, 1984).
11. D. Lee Bawden and John L. Palmer, "Social Policy: Challenging the Welfare State," in John L. Palmer and Isabel V. Sawhill, eds. *The Reagan Record* (Cambridge, MA: Ballinger Publishing, 1984), p. 365.
12. See *Annual Educational Summary, 1988-89*, (Albany: Information Center on Education, State Education Department, 1990), Table 22, p. 27.
13. "Texas Judge Backs Law on School Aid," *New York Times*, April 16, 1991.
14. See Jeanne Reock and Michael Kaelber, Esq., "The Quality Education Act of 1990: A Board Member's Guide," New Jersey School

Boards Association, Trenton, N.J., 1990.
15. See *Abbott v. Burke*, 119 N.J. 287, 575 A, 2d 358 (1990).
16. "Florio School Aid Cut; Homeowners Get Tax Relief," *New York Times*, March 12, 1991.
17. "Bush Unveils Education Bill Calling for Parental Choice," *New York Times*, April 19, 1991.

6.
EQUAL EDUCATIONAL OPPORTUNITY VERSUS THE REALITIES OF AMERICAN SOCIETY

It is repugnant to the idea of equal educational opportunity that the quality of a child's education, insofar as that education is provided through public funds, is determined by accidents of birth, wealth, or geography; that a child who lives in a poor district is, by reason of that fact alone, entitled to lower public investment in his education than a child in a rich district. It is unconscionable that a poor man in a poor district must often pay local taxes at higher rates for the inferior education of his child than the man of means in a rich district pays for the superior education of his child.

—The Fleischmann Report

The previous chapters have focused on a variety of subjects, all with the purpose of clarifying the reasons that the struggle for greater educational opportunity, in terms of either equality or equity, has been so limited in its results. We analyzed philosophical concepts, historical experiences, the reasons reform efforts were limited in impact, the manner in which the legislative process undermines reform, the generally discouraging attempts at judicial reform, and current developments on the American political scene which are likely to limit changes in the future.

In this closing chapter we shall concern ourselves with what we have learned about American ideals, values and practices as a result of concentration on the issue of equality of educational opportunity. This is not meant to imply some notion of a general theory of American democracy demonstrated by the study; our ambitions are far more modest. Our concern is with how the conflicts and struggles described reflect the basic tensions and conflicts of American society. Our analysis of educational finance leads us to pose broader questions about our society; these questions in turn lead us to a deepened appreciation for the complexities of educational finance reform.

Local Control and State Policies

Regarding the governance and control of education, local control is a prime value in America and is equated with liberty. This is reflected in the power of local residents to elect a school board and also to regularly approve or reject school budgets. A rationale of this special treatment is that more than any other governmental function, education is related directly to the immediate concerns of the community and the family. However, developments over the last decades have resulted in greater state powers of regulation and control over education, eliminating thereby many of the prerogatives traditionally associated with local control and independence.

Although the citizenry continues to regard schools as the last haven of local autonomy, that haven has in fact become a much molested sanctuary. For a price, independent local school districts have been willing to terminate their separate existence. Consolidation of school districts in New York State and elsewhere was made possible only through the offer of generous state subsidies, which enticed districts to surrender their separate status. During the period between 1931-32 and 1987-88, the number of school districts in the nation declined from 127,531 to 15,577.[1] In New York State, there has been a reduction from 10,000 districts around the turn of the century to 721 in 1988-89.[2]

Despite a significant diminution in local authority and control, the unique fiscal independence of school districts is still a status that is prized. But, local resources are not the sole support of school finance and, without significant state aid, many districts would not be able to function. Local control has become a slogan for the protection of local privilege and maintenance of the status quo, even though many of these localities are dependent on state support for their existence. Attempts to move to larger scales of organization that would curtail this independence are fiercely resisted.

In the same manner that localism and community control may conflict with proposals for reform and change, conflicts in basic values are intensified by the opposing tendencies involved in liberty and equality. A justification of the exisiting system of school governance is that it favors community involvement and local control. A criticism of this system is that it encourages and maintains disparities and inequalities that resist attempts at amelioration by larger governing bodies.

To the extent that reformers and the state pursue goals of redistribution and equality, they oppose claims at the local level for greater independence. Conflicts between local school districts and state governments thus become battles waged under competing ideological banners of equality and liberty. Greater equality cannot be obtained unless there is more intervention by the state to impose limits to local authority. Local independence and control may conflict with attempts by the state to pursue more equality. American democracy is replete with other examples of the conflict between these opposing interests. The tendency at present is toward less reliance on central government initiatives and greater recognition of local perogatives.

The Impact of Equity on Social Stability

Educational reformers place goals of equality and equity at the top of their hierachy of values, arguing that it is the responsibility of society to redistribute resources to enlarge educational opportunity for those who are less fortunate. This entails conflict with the interests of those who benefit from the existing situation. Resources are always limited and attempts to increase assistance to one group will be resisted by others who fear less attention will be given to their needs.

Equality cannot be attained through good intentions. The struggle can only succeed under conditions of strain and challenge to the social and political system. Those who seek equality do so out of a conviction that it represents a prime social value and reflects the highest level of social justice and morality. However, the more intensely equality is pursued, the more disruptive will be the consequences.

Societies often face shifts between times of stability and accommodation as opposed to periods of intense agitation and dislocation. During the 1960s, American education was one of a number of areas where long-entrenched inequalities were being challenged. Great social instability resulted, with increased political conflict and discord. A reaction to the ferment of the 1960s has resulted in a moderation of expectations regarding social change. Equality of educational opportunity is another issue which has receded from public interest, as concerns with stability and order take precedence over ideals regarding justice and equality.

The Changing Face of Inequality

The problem of educational inequalities related to local property wealth disparities dates back to the beginning of public schooling. What is new is the pattern of its present incidence. Historically, the major element of inequality affecting the public financing of education was based upon rural-urban wealth differentials, with increasing differences resulting from the concentration of commercial and industrial wealth in the large, rapidly developing industrial cities.

As major concentrations of wealth shifted to the central business districts in the cities, rural areas were increasingly disadvantaged in their ability to raise revenues for schools. With the development of a commitment to free public education, a major mission of state government was to remedy these disparities through various educational aid formulas. However, because of the then existing legislative malapportionment, rural areas were often able to secure favorable legislation, which garnered for them disproportionate shares of state aid.

The contemporary face of inequality is different. Succinctly, it may be described as the dispersion of class and race over space and place. The evolution of urbanization, from the inital concentration in the industrial central city to the spread metropolis, has been accompanied by a non-random sorting out and dispersion of the population along both racial and class lines. The gradual dispersion of economic activity from the central business districts to suburban areas along with the residential shift of the more affluent population groups has intensified the inequality between city and suburban areas.

As a result of this metropolitanization process, school districts reflect the class and racial divisions of the larger urban society. The central city, previously more affluent and advantaged, has become increasingly disadvantaged because of the phenomenon of "municipal overburden." The central-city poor have greater needs for governmental services, while the more affluent in the suburban ring have significantly less dependence upon governmental support. Because of the mismatch of needs and resources, cities with overburden find themselves spending a larger proportion of their revenues on non-educational services, while suburban areas are able to concentrate their attention on public schools. This has resulted in suburban school districts becoming increasingly advantaged in comparision with other urban and rural districts.

The racial aspects of this phenomenon are especially important, because of the linkage between poverty and race in the United States. Poor blacks and Hispanics are concentrated in the central city with its underfunded and underachieving school system. The more affluent white population attends better funded schools with significantly higher rates of student achievement. Earlier state efforts were concentrated on remedying disparities between white urban and rural populations; the current situation is exacerbated the segregation of racial minoritities in city schools.

Attempts to significantly reduce inequalities and to develop special educational programs are bound to be resisted by a threatened white majority who oppose special treatment of minority groups. This majority has the political muscle to thwart attempts to redistribute resources. This is why it is so difficult to achieve significant progress toward equality of educational opportunity. The issue is too vital, immediate and central; the stakes are too high; and the participants use their knowledge of the political system to protect their interests with competence and intensity.

The Problem of the Single Issue Coalition

In Chapters 3 and 4, we speculated on ways in which more successful coalitions for educational reform might be formed. Absent from our discussion was the importance of racial factors in limiting the effectiveness of such coalitions. As long as the cities of America are perceived as identical to the interests of blacks and other minority students, it is more difficult to form a coalition that will combine city interests with those of rural and less affluent urban areas. This is true nationally, but especially in New York State, where the five major cities all have dependent school districts, a factor which creates a different set of political and budgetary calculations. More state educational aid to the cities is viewed in many parts of the state as another form of general fiscal relief rather than special educational aid, since there is no clear guarantee (as in the case of independent school districts) that additional funds for the cities will actually be spent on education.

The fact that New York City alone contains 77 percent of the total of all black and Hispanic students in the state, and that New York City and the rest of the Big Five total 84 percent of all such students,[3] undermines the commonality of interests that might have unified cities with other needier parts of the state. The traditional animosity of upstate urban and rural areas to the big cities has now taken on a new character—the additional factor of color, which serves to further isolate cities and reduce possibilities for formation of a broad coalition for educational equality.

Education as a "Non-political" Issue

The emphasis throughout this book has been on analyzing those factors that prevent the achievement of equality of educational expenditures in the financing of public education. We have attempted to break away from tendencies of reformers, practitioners and technicians to emphasize the more formal aspects of the structure of school finance, by focusing on revision and manipulation of state educational aid formulas to achieve more equalizing results. Although this approach is important, we believe that such an emphasis has tended to limit our understanding of the process, creating an illusion that change is best achieved through such technical adjustments.

The tendency to view education separately from politics is based upon the idea that education is different, belonging to a neutral domain of professional concern and attention that distinguishes it from the intensity of conflict that characterizes the political process. This has encouraged viewing education as a special sector of public allocation, separate from politics and the machinations that intrude upon all other aspects of public resource allocation. This notion of "specialness" is reflected in the American approach to educational policy and has been a source of legitimization of the special district system of educational governance. It also serves as the justification for holding special "nonpartisan" elections for school district officers, and for the submission of school budgets for voter approval.

Because it involves the interests of children and society in a unique manner, education was intended to be kept separate and apart from "the contaminating influences of politics." This orientation has been supported by local communities and professional associations as a justification for maintenance of the current system. This "uniqueness" has actually served as a cover, however, for the intense politicization of education in this country, obfuscating the fact that public education is as political as any other activity of government, and usually more complex, relating as it does to the smallest and largest units of society, from the individual, family and community to local, state and federal governments. Conflicts regarding educational policy have been especially intense over the last two decades, and we have sought to emphasize the intensely political nature of the struggle for educational opportunity.

Changing Prospects for Equality

The struggle for educational equality relates to all aspects of the social and political system. Hope among reformers has in the past been raised by new developments. The passage of a more promising equalizing aid formula by state government; a commitment by the federal government to policies of compensatory education; hope for increasing consolidation of local school districts; and expectations of judicial rulings by federal and state courts that would expand fundamental rights doctrines to public education—all of these factors and many more were responsible for gains made during the 1960s and the subsequent optimism regarding future developments. Recent reversals in all of these areas have since resulted in pessimism regarding future prospects for equality of educational opportunity.

This is but a part of the larger picture of political change that has been taking place in the nation, reflected in the shift from redistributive, equity-oriented policies to retrenchment and the rejection of such a strong governmental role. Education is subject to the same pressures and constraints as other programs. The erosion of the welfare state has undermined a commitment to redistribution and compensatory programs that would equalize opportunity for poor and minority children. Especially affected have been poor school districts since they are the most dependent on aid from other sources. Because the root of the resource problem is at the local level, the only hope for change is through aggressive intervention by state and federal governments. The rejection of such a role undermines expectations of any significant change.

The striving for equality cannot proceed in a vacuum; it requires nurturing by a set of interrelated factors. A growing and strong economy is an underlying prerequisite—a basis for the spirit of generosity that is required to mobilize public support. Also the climate of opinion must be such that it encourages a broad sense of compassion and hope regarding the desirability of governmental policies to aid the disadvantaged. Without such a societal consensus, special treatment of any group quickly loses favor and will not long be tolerated, especially if this group is perceived as a distinct minority.

The collapse of the relatively brief consensus regarding compensatory education demonstrates the fragile nature of the political support for such policies in this country. American society is highly dynamic and volatile, possessed of a short attention span and impatient with slow and uncertain results, hardly a hospitable nurturing ground for educational programs responding to the needs of the poor, especially when they are perceived by many as conflicting with the interests and needs of their own children.

The Legislative Process as a Limit to Change

Regardless of the political climate of opinion and the balance of forces at any one time, institutional structures may set constraints that limit speedy and dramatic change. The legislative process is an ideal place for delaying and diluting intensive political movement of any kind. Its daily existence is tied to discussion, debate and delay; its decisions reflect conference, compromise and consensus; and the harsh measure of political success against which each legislator is measured is the goal of re-election.

The fact that re-election is indeed the prime pursuit of each legislator imposes a discipline and restraint upon operations, forcing outcomes that avoid extremes. The political consequences of every vote makes the legislator more responsive to local needs and pressures rather than to broader considerations of the larger public interest. Since educational aid is a critical recurring issue on the legislative calendar, the leadership must regularly forge coalitions that will result in decisions that do not undermine and isolate party members.

The essential dynamic of the legislature is compromise and restraint in order to delay and moderate the intensity of pressures for radical change and create thereby a basis for greater consensus that will not threaten large numbers of the membership, or the coalitions and group interests which they represent. The legislative process moderates the intensity of different demands, especially regarding issues of state educational aid, where equalization proposals might otherwise cause great conflict by pitting poor and affluent school districts against each other.

In Search of the Public Interest

Legislative decisions reflect the pressure of local interests, the views of which can only be ignored at the peril of each elected official—especially regarding such a critical issue as school aid. Because of the nature of bargaining and coalition forming within and between the two parties and houses, local interests are an especially important and determining factor. What is more difficult to articulate, however, is a perception of the general public interest and how this might best be served.

Edmund Burke, in his letters to Bristol, written more than two centuries ago, stated the conflict that confronts legislators and undermines their ability to respond to a larger public interest. His views of that time are clearly applicable to the manner in which legislatures function in contemporary America. Representatives must decide whether in parliamentary votes they should act as "delegates," disregarding their own personal views and instead representing the desires of their constituents, or, as "trustees," formulating positions based on their evaluation of the facts as related to the public good, even in those cases where doing so would bring them into conflict with their own constituents. Burke strongly advocated the trustee model of representation, arguing that it was the responsibility of representatives to think not only of the interests of their district, but first and foremost of the general good of the larger community. This orientation led Burke to follow the dictates of his conscience during his tenure as a member of Parliament from Bristol and was an important factor in the early termination of his legislative career.[4]

Burke's analysis of conflictual legislative role models is especially relevant to an understanding of the politics of the struggle for equality of educational opportunity. The prime goal of legislators is to be reelected. Unlike some issues, where there may be tolerance for deviation, on matters of state educational aid, legislators *must* vote the interests of their local constituents if they wish to be reelected, even though many may believe that the larger interest of society would best be served by voting in another way. Many legislators know that the greatest need for state educational aid exists in poor rural and big city areas, and that the public interest would best be served by responding to that need. But considerations of political survival compel voting decisions that place local considerations ahead of the larger public interest.

In Chapter 3, we mentioned that the political nature of the legislative decision-making process precludes significant progress toward equality of educational opportunity. Because of these limits, we recommended in Chapter 5 that powers for the determining the allocation process of state educational aid be turned over to an "expert non-political body,"which would be better able to formulate decisions in terms of the larger public interest. Regardless of the mechanism that is developed to pursue this goal, it seems clear that the current situation of political determination by the legislature guarantees that the public interest, while prominently proclaimed in the platitudes of public pronouncements, will regularly be displaced by the more immediate concerns of individual legislators, who must satisfy local interests in order to be reelected.

Commissions and Studies, Professors and Experts

In Chapter 2, we mentioned the various special studies, task forces and commissions that have been created to consider questions of state aid. Many of these groups have been of blue ribbon quality, and have been endowed with great financial support that enabled the hiring of large staffs. They have had access to outside academic and consultant talent, along with the support facilities of the governmental bureaucracy. This provides legitimacy and public acceptability and, to the extent that efforts are coordinated with the bureaucracy, a more sympathetic reception is ensured for its subsequent findings. Many impressive reports have been written, volumes of which fill the shelves of the state library system. Most often, the greatest attention accorded these studies has been the effort required to cart them to their final resting place.

The reports, although spread over a period of more than seventy years, read almost as if written by the same hand. They contain a statement of the problem, analysis of the root causes and suggestions for remedy. Essentially, the recommendations for action have remained the same. What has changed is the degree of glitter and gloss accompanying each report. The quality of paper, binding and product preparation have also improved significantly. Another enhancement is the impressive array of statistical information flowing from the latest computer technology. Recent products, such as those of the Fleischmann and Rubin Commissions, are the most impressive in format and style, but their analysis and recommendations are little different from that of past commissions.

For a long time there has been unanimity regarding the magnitude of existing disparities, and the need to change existing laws to achieve greater equality. Some commissions have urged consolidation of school districts so as to reduce the extremes of wealth and poverty associated with small districts; others have called for redesigning the system of school governance in order to make the county the locus of a school district. Some have called for removing all financing responsibility from local school districts and implementing total state asumption of that function. Other reports have been more modest in their recommendations, concerned less with comprehensive structural changes than with technical manipulations in the state aid formula or with revisions of educational law.

The need to appoint new commissions occurs when problems reach a crisis level and are not capable of being addressed immediately through the political process. The tactic of appointing commissions and study groups is used by both legislative and executive branches to shift the focus of attention to research and long-term analysis, thereby postponing the call for immediate action to a time when it is hoped that passions will have subsided. This approach is sanctified by reliance upon a neutral, non-political outside body of disinterested professionals, a measure that involves both cost and delay. Cost is a small matter if it purchases time and dilutes the intensity of pressures for change. This is not to say that commissions have no impact; they do, but only in a context of incremental change that does not go beyond the boundaries of political acceptability. Regardless of the variety of recommendation, the most important function of commissions is to legitimize the authority of the political process and to provide a breathing space which enables the political system to function.

Frances Kemmerer in her article, "The Role of Commissions in School Finance Reform in New York," assesses the situation in a succinct if somewhat contradictory manner:

> A superficial review of finance commissions in New York State leads one to suspect that, whatever role they were designed to play in policy making, commissions had little effect on the decisions taken. Both the issues addressed by the earliest commissions and the recommendations they made are hauntingly familiar to those who have followed the Rubin Task Force efforts. This is not to say, however, that they had no effect on legislative outcomes. The state share in the cost of local schooling has risen steadily over the past sixty years and the increases have generally reflected commission recommendations. It is to say that there has never been a clear victory for reformers. The

structural problems which lie at the heart of taxpayer and student inequities have never been resolved.[5]

The realities of school finance dictate outcomes that are at great
variance with the comprehensive reform proposals of commissions and
study groups. Some incremental changes and tinkering modifications
of the formula are adopted by the legislature. But the basic root
problems are not attended to, as the essential message of these proposals
is covered over, only to be resurrected at a later date by yet another study
group.

Our discussion regarding commissions and task forces would be
incomplete, especially on the part of two professors, if we concluded
without mention of the enhanced attention and power given to professionals, professors and technicians—the so-called "experts"—whose
special knowledge plays a central role in this process. It is not that the
experts dominate decision makers; in fact, their actual influence is far
less than might be inferred from the media attention they receive.

Issues regarding state aid to education are too closely tied to local
communities and the political survival of legislators for much support
to be given to the untrammeled findings of experts. However, simply
when viewed in terms of magnitude, the role of experts has increased
significantly—in cost, numbers of people involved, breadth of research,
sophistication of data development, styles of presentation and also in
enhanced recognition and prestige for those participants. Consultants
have become a central element in the political combat involving war-
ring numbers and disputed findings, which are used by contending
groups to advance their interests. And with new developments in com-
puters and information processing, there is an increasing reliance upon
the printout as the continually revised and updated scoreboard showing
winners and losers from legislative proposals, a tally closely scrutinized
by all legislators.

Competence with such information has greatly enhanced the role
of staff and technicians. In the pre-computer age, decisions regarding
aid formulas were negotiated among the leadership, and members simply followed party discipline. Individual members relied on the leadership and staff to negotiate in their best interests and very few understood
the details involved. Laborious computations had to be made before
members became aware of the impact of a new law on their own district. The results were available too late to affect the individual
member's vote or to allow for pressure upon the leadership for change.

However, now in the computer age, there are far more staff and technicians, and each member has access to the latest printouts, which arrive while proposals are actually being negotiated. Members can then determine exactly how the new aid formula will affect their districts, and exert themselves to change those results. Consequently, greater accessibility to information and data reduces the power of the leadership to impose policies on their conferences without first mediating and resolving differences. At the same time, the power of each individual member is enhanced because greater knowledge encourages more participation in decision making.

The impact of this on the struggle for equality is many-sided. It is true that reformers and equality advocates can more effectively marshal data to demonstrate inequities in the system. However, a statement and diagnosis of the problem does not necessarily lead to a resolution, especially when the availability of data enables all to perceive clearly how proposals will affect their interests. Information and computerization have a double edge—greater knowledge to challenge the system but also enhanced power to maintain the status quo against reform, especially because the legislature depends upon negotiated compromises and deals to form coalitions for conference majorities in each house. Because of these factors and other matters discussed in more detail in Chapter 3, greater member access to information and data is likely to increase resistance to attempts at reform.

The development and distribution of information technology is by no means a neutral element in the political process. The experts themselves, along with the information they develop and present, have become an increasingly important part of the process of conflict and mediation.They are used by different groups for different purposes, as all sides rely on different sets of experts to justify their competing viewpoints. Often, commissions and study groups rely upon academic experts who are brought in as consultants.

However, it seems that in regard to issues of educational equality, the findings of the experts have been far more weighty than their impact. They are more often the tail being wagged by the dictates of legislative desires. They are an important part of the process, but do not have a major role in decisions regarding equality. Their role is usually restricted to the particularities of formula changes and special impacts. Although styles of political combat have changed, the broad parameters of decision making, and hence the results, remain under the control of the leadership.

Equity and Equality in American Democracy

A central element of American democracy has been the idea of opportunity for all citizens, regardless of racial, religious or ethnic differences. In fact, protection against such discrimination is a part of those fundamental rights guaranteed by federal and most state constitutions. More controversial, and not defined as a fundamental, constitutionally protected right, is the protection against inequality of opportunity resulting from wealth differences. Much political conflict stems from the struggle to define a greater governmental responsibility to increase educational opportunity as disadvantaged groups seek to expand their participation in American society.

Although equality of educational opportunity is not a constitutionally protected right, the provision of education is a central responsibility of state governments. Universal free schooling is provided in all states. Furthermore, the social ethos of society includes a notion of justice that dictates a governmental responsibility to pursue educational policies that enlarge educational opportunity for all children. While some educational policies accomplish this purpose, the exisiting situation is, nevertheless, far from the ideals of equality and equity that we have discussed in Chapter 1 and other parts of this book.

The political system, as reflected in state legislatures across the country, and in most cases the judicial system (federal and the majority of the states), have rejected ideals of equity and equality as being the standard for determining educational policy. However, the argument is by no means settled and remains an issue of perennial concern and conflict.

Educational opportunity is an issue too closely related to fundamental social, community and individual interests to be removed from the center of political conflict. Despite the continual agitation, however, it seems unlikely that proponents of equality-equity standards will be successful in their struggle for a radical reinterpretation of the American system. For what is involved in the quest of reformers are changes in policies that go to the heart of the society, affecting the basic elements of power and privilege as they relate to family and community.

Progress toward equality of educational opportunity threatens and undermines basic relationships of class and status, which are at the heart of society. Wealthier parents will fight for the right to spend as much as they wish for the education of their children, thereby generating levels of educational expenditures that would be impossible for society to maintain for all children. The more privileged will also resist leveling attempts to limit their educational expenditures as a method of reducing inequalities. If poor districts get more state aid, richer districts are able to raise far more revenue than poorer districts. As a result, while all districts may experience at least some improvement, the disparities among school districts will grow even larger. Essentially, that is the message of American democracy: the provision of an educational opportunity, but within circumscribed limits that stop far short of equality or equity. How far short? That is what the political process is all about.

The Continuing Struggle

> They cannot vote yet; they are yet incompletely educated and quite inexperienced. Many are only beginning to learn to read and write. They are still wet and stand upon wobbly legs. They know not the way, so we must lead them. They know not how, so we must show them. . . . The facts that I have recited and found indicate that our financial system, which includes the combination of state and local funds as they currently act in tandem, do not yet meet the requirements of our constitution. With all due respect to history and the legislature for its recent generous and thoughtful efforts to rectify this situation, by order of this Court the current system will be set aside.[6]

* * *

> There is no equality of educational opportunity in America. But there is an opportunity.[7]

We have in this book chronicled a story of more than a century to achieve greater equality of educational opportunity in New York State. We have described those factors which prevent significant progress toward equalization of educational opportunity in New York State, now and in the foreseeable future. Progress toward educational opportunity, by seeking special treatment for the most disadvantaged groups, alienates many who feel their interests threatened. This creates reactions that result in greater desire for stability and maintenance of the status quo.

While at times, as in the 1960s, there was more hope that progress might be made, such is not the current situation. As we discussed in Chapter 4, the United States Supreme Court and the New York State Court of Appeals have essentially closed off the judicial avenue of redress. The possibilites for legislative action are restricted to at best minimal responses to inequality, which although improving the situation of poor districts is not going to reduce inequalities.

We have at a number of points in this book criticized the tendencies of reformers and academicians to focus on state aid formula reforms. While this work is important, we believe that the realities of party politics and legislative decision making, and not deficiencies in aid formulas, are the major factors that limit progress toward this goal.

The only way to achieve equality of educational opportunity, as defined in the fiscal sense, is through basic fundamental reform of the institutional structure for educational policy making. This means reasserting once more the findings of earlier educational finance theorists who understood clearly that significant change could not take place as long as there was a mismatch between the incidence of poor children and the property wealth tax base of a community. We believe that equality cannot be achieved unless there is a total state takeover of educational finance, which will eliminate local property and income wealth differences as determinants of school expenditures. In this way, the issue that has dominated state politics for over a century will finally be resolved.

We know how unlikely it is that such change will take place in New York State, especially now that pressures from legal challenges have subsided. We expect that the current situation will continue, with educational finance being a major focus of state political and legislative activity, and with continuing conflict over the distribution of state aid to local districts. The aid formula will continue to be the center of attention as the symbolism of equalization camouflages and obfuscates the realities of political decision making.

But the durability and perennial nature of this issue will be certain to force its resurfacing. Goals of equality and opportunity, although often viewed as divergent and conflicting ideals, have found a common nesting ground in the controversies of school finance. For there is something about this system that violates basic American standards of decency and fair play in a way that goes beyond ordinary political arrangements and compromises.

There is a sense of shock and revulsion that many experience when confronted with the reality that the American governmental system discriminates among the children of the wealthy and the poor in the provision of resources for public schooling. Certainly many, especially in the more affluent and suburban areas, benefit from this arrangement and will continue to resist attempts to change the status quo. But few will defend it as representing the better side of American democracy.

Even in the most favorable of circumstances, the struggle for educational equality is in conflict with some of the most entrenched values and institutional forces of society. But despite the fact that there is now little hope for progress, one can still anticipate the continuation of political struggle. Ideals of equality are central to the democratic creed and part of the social contract which holds out the promise of opportunity to all persons. It is precisely when opportunity seems most clearly denied that one can once again look to the resurrection of the ideal as a means of mobilizing support and power on the part of disadvantaged groups. For that is the essence of the history of American democracy, the struggle for the realization of its promise for an increasing number of its citizenry.

The historical enlargement of human rights under American democracy is described by Joseph Alsop in his centennial biography of Franklin Roosevelt:

> At the time of Franklin Delano Roosevelt's inauguration close to fifty percent of all Americans were in some degree excluded from the full rights enjoyed by all WASP Americans (except for those few living in ancient, isolated pockets of primitivism and poverty, like the Appalachian mountain people). More particularly, non-WASP Americans, however able, were excluded from the normal opportunities of any moderately fortunate WASP. In some cases, the exclusion was downright shocking, as with the blacks and the Americans of Asian origin. But in all cases the exclusion was there, whether in greater or lesser measure, and it was felt and bitterly resented. To Roosevelt, therefore, about forty percent of all Americans now owe the fact that they have become undoubted 'citizens with a full share'. . . . This gigantic achievement prepared the way for the long effort, still happily in progress, to give a full share to those who remain partly excluded . . . although Franklin Roosevelt did not finish the job.[8]

This book has dealt with an unfinished part of that task, the attempt to provide equality of educational opportunity for poor children, most of whom are members of those minority groups.

Perhaps, in spite of the valiant efforts of more than a century, that is the best that America will now provide for many of its poorest and most disadvantaged children. However, it is always difficult to project the trends of tomorrow from the tendencies of today. Changing circumstances may result one day in a different tale. The harbingers of continuing ferment are already evident in the statement of Judge Harley Clark, cited earlier, in his ruling striking down the Texas system of educational finance as being a violation of fundamental rights.

Issues and conflicts regarding equality and equity are bound to endure as permanent features of American society. We hope this book has stimulated interest and concern regarding the importance of this subject and also contributed to understanding the underlying realities that determine outcomes in educational finance.

NOTES

1. *Digest of Educational Statistics 1989* (Washington, DC: National Center for Educational Statistics, U.S. Office of Education, 1989), Table 79, p. 90.
2. *Annual Educational Summary, 1988-89* (Albany: Information Center on Education, New York State Education Department, 1989), Table 3, p. 5.
3. Ibid., Table 18, p. 21.
4. For a detailed discussion of this subject's importance in the life of Burke, see Ernest Barker, *Burke and Bristol: A Study of the Relations Between Burke and His Constituency During the Years 1774-1780* (Bristol, England: Arrowsmith Publishers, 1931).
5. Frances Kemmerrer, "The Role of Commissions in School Finance Reform in New York," *The Council Journal* 1, No. 5 (March 1983), p. 55.
6. Opinion of Judge Harley Clark, District Judge, State of Texas, in *Edgewood Independent School District v. Kirby* (April 29, 1975).
7. From the reflections of David Yeefon, Hunter College undergraduate student (a parking lot attendant working his way through college) in one of the author's classes.
8. Joseph Alsop, *FDR: Centenary Remembrance* (New York: Viking Press, 1982), pp.12-13.

STATISTICAL APPENDIX

Table 1
REVENUES FOR PUBLIC ELEMENTARY AND SECONDARY SCHOOLS BY SOURCE OF FUNDS, U.S.A.: 1919-20 TO 1986-87

School year	In thousands				Percentage distribution			
	Total	Federal	State	Local (including intermediate)[1]	Total	Federal	State	Local (including intermediate)[1]
1	2	3	4	5	6	7	8	9
1919-20	$970,121	$2,475	$160,085	$807,561	100.0	0.3	16.5	83.2
1929-30	2,088,557	7,334	353,670	1,727,553	100.0	0.4	16.9	82.7
1939-40	2,260,527	39,810	684,354	1,536,363	100.0	1.8	30.3	68.0
1941-42	2,416,580	34,305	759,993	1,622,281	100.0	1.4	31.4	67.1
1943-44	2,604,322	35,886	859,183	1,709,253	100.0	1.4	33.0	65.6
1945-46	3,059,845	41,378	1,062,057	1,956,409	100.0	1.4	34.7	63.9
1947-48	4,311,534	120,270	1,676,362	2,514,902	100.0	2.8	38.9	58.3
1949-50	5,437,044	155,848	2,165,689	3,115,507	100.0	2.9	39.8	57.3
1951-52	6,423,816	227,711	2,478,596	3,717,507	100.0	3.5	38.6	57.9
1953-54	7,866,852	355,237	2,944,103	4,567,512	100.0	4.5	37.4	58.1
1955-56	9,686,677	441,442	3,828,886	5,416,350	100.0	4.6	39.5	55.9
1957-58	12,181,513	486,484	4,800,368	6,894,661	100.0	4.0	39.4	56.6
1959-60	14,746,618	651,639	5,768,047	8,326,932	100.0	4.4	39.1	56.5
1961-62	17,527,707	760,975	6,789,190	9,977,542	100.0	4.3	38.7	56.9
1963-64	20,544,182	896,956	8,078,014	11,569,213	100.0	4.4	39.3	56.3
1965-66	25,356,858	1,996,954	9,920,219	13,439,686	100.0	7.9	39.1	53.0
1967-68	31,903,064	2,806,469	12,275,536	16,821,063	100.0	8.8	38.5	52.7
1969-70	40,266,923	3,219,557	16,062,776	20,984,589	100.0	8.0	39.9	52.1
1970-71	44,511,292	3,753,461	17,409,086	23,348,745	100.0	8.4	39.1	52.5
1971-72	50,003,645	4,467,969	19,133,256	26,402,420	100.0	8.9	38.3	52.8

Table 1 - continued

Year							
1972–73	52,117,930	4,525,000	20,843,520	26,749,412	100.0	8.7	40.0	51.3
1973–74	58,230,892	4,930,351	24,113,409	29,187,132	100.0	8.5	41.4	50.1
1974–75	64,445,239	5,811,595	27,211,116	31,422,528	100.0	9.0	42.2	48.8
1975–76	71,206,073	6,318,345	31,776,101	33,111,627	100.0	8.9	44.6	46.5
1976–77	75,322,532	6,629,498	32,688,903	36,004,134	100.0	8.8	43.4	47.8
1977–78	81,443,160	7,694,194	35,013,266	38,735,700	100.0	9.4	43.0	47.6
1978–79	87,994,143	8,600,116	40,132,136	39,261,891	100.0	9.8	45.6	44.6
1979–80	96,881,165	9,503,537	45,348,814	42,028,813	100.0	9.8	46.8	43.4
1980–81	105,949,087	9,768,262	50,182,659	45,998,166	100.0	9.2	47.4	43.4
1981–82	110,191,257	8,186,466	52,436,435	49,568,356	100.0	7.4	47.6	45.0
1982–83	117,497,502	8,339,990	56,282,157	52,875,354	100.0	7.1	47.9	45.0
1983–84	126,055,419	8,576,547	60,232,981	57,245,892	100.0	6.8	47.8	45.4
1984–85	137,294,678	9,105,569	67,168,684	61,020,425	100.0	6.6	48.9	44.4
1985–86²	149,127,779	9,975,622	73,619,575	65,532,582	100.0	6.7	49.4	43.9
1986–87	158,827,473	10,145,899	79,022,572	69,659,003	100.0	6.4	49.8	43.9

¹Includes a relatively small amount from nongovernmental sources (gifts, tuition and transportation fees from patrons). These sources accounted for 0.4 percent of total revenues in 1967
²Revised from previously published figures.

NOTES—Beginning in 1980–81, revenues for state education agencies are excluded. Because of rounding details may not add to totals.

SOURCE: U.S. Department of Education, National Center for Education Statistics, *Statistics of State School Systems: Revenues and Expenditures for Public Elementary and Secondary Education*, Table 138, p. 48; and Common Core of Data survey. (This table was prepared November 1988.)

Table 2
NEW YORK STATE PUBLIC SCHOOL REVENUE FROM FEDERAL, STATE AND LOCAL SOURCES: 1972-73 TO 1989-90[a] (In Thousands)

| School Year | Total General & Special Aid Fund Expenditures | STATE AID | |
		Amount	Percent of Total Expenditures
1989-90[c]	$19,038,000[d]	$7,870,000[d]	41.3%
1989-90[c]	19,722,000[e]	8,554,000[e]	43.4
1988-89[f]	18,317,000	8,095,000	44.2
1987-88	16,885,750	7,391,573	43.8
1986-87	15,461,097	6,663,866	43.1
1985-86	14,456,668	6,001,342	41.5
1984-85	13,244,994	5,483,139	41.4
1983-84	12,414,761	4,876,658	39.3
1982-83	11,549,609	4,644,808	40.2
1981-82	10,879,138	4,272,493	39.3
1980-81	9,969,092	3,957,793	39.7
1979-80	9,239,986	3,595,147	38.9
1978-79	8,687,679	3,367,330	38.8
1977-78	8,353,195	3,142,598	37.6
1976-77	7,901,601	3,094,494	39.2
1975-76	7,624,134	3,069,968	40.3
1974-75	7,392,526	2,922,894	39.5
1973-74	6,675,067	2,551,037	38.2
1972-73	5,969,276	2,439,707	40.9

[a] For school years 1961-62 to 1971-72, the reader is referred to the *Analysis of School Finances in New York State School Districts, 1979-80,* Albany: State Education Department, 1981.

[b] Includes all local property and nonproperty tax balances carried forward from previous years as well as miscellaneous revenues in current year. This is a balancing amount since the table assumes all other revenues were expended in the year received.

Table 2 - continued

FEDERAL AID		LOCAL TAX & OTHER REVENUES[b]	
Amount	Percent of Total Expenditures	Amount	Percent of Total Expenditures
$560,000	3.0%	$10,608,000	55.7%
560,000	2.8	10,608,000	53.8
570,000	3.1	9,652,000	52.7
497,882	2.9	8,996,295	53.3
498,217	3.2	8,299,014	53.7
584,832	4.0	7,870,494	54.5
443,279	3.3	7,318,576	55.3
448,000	3.6	7,090,103	57.1
446,000	3.9	6,458,801	55.9
426,551	3.9	6,180,094	56.8
473,175	4.8	5,538,124	55.5
503,492	5.4	5,141,347	55.7
420,212	4.9	4,900,137	56.3
387,813	4.6	4,822,784	57.8
339,055	4.3	4,468,052	56.5
335,571	4.4	4,218,595	55.3
375,773	5.1	4,093,859	55.4
275,728	4.1	3,848,302	57.7
292,717	4.9	3,236,852	54.2

[c] Estimated.
[d] With TRS maximum deduct of $684 million; does not include possible prepayment by individual school districts.
[e] Anticipated prior to deferral of 1989-90 TRS payments.
[f] Preliminary.

SOURCE: New York State Education Department, Albany, New York.

Table 3

PUBLIC ELEMENTARY AND SECONDARY SCHOOL REVENUE BY SOURCE AND STATE: 1986-87

(In Thousands)

State or other area	Total	Revenues, by source					
		Federal		State		Local and other[1]	
		Amount	Percent of total	Amount	Percent of total	Amount	Percent of total
1	2	3	4	5	6	7	8
United States[2]	$158,827,473	$10,145,899	6.4	$79,022,572	49.8	$69,659,003	43.9
Alabama	2,070,639	241,402	11.7	1,372,963	66.3	456,274	22.0
Alaska	731,150	85,277	11.7	465,599	63.7	180,274	24.7
Arizona	2,106,564	189,004	9.0	1,017,425	48.3	900,134	42.7
Arkansas	1,111,619	128,173	11.5	608,757	54.8	374,689	33.7
California	17,219,479	1,217,998	7.1	11,961,834	69.5	4,039,647	23.5
Colorado	2,395,723	117,590	4.9	935,154	39.0	1,342,978	56.1
Connecticut	2,606,381	114,873	4.4	1,043,373	40.0	1,448,136	55.6
Delaware	429,392	32,998	7.7	297,291	69.2	99,103	23.1
District of Columbia	439,795	45,460	10.3	2,725	0.6	391,610	89.0
Florida	6,610,567	475,228	7.2	3,581,688	54.2	2,553,651	38.6
Georgia	3,708,383	263,083	7.1	2,213,166	59.7	1,232,134	33.2
Hawaii	592,815	70,191	11.8	522,096	88.1	528	0.1
Idaho	544,525	48,203	8.9	342,286	62.9	154,036	28.3
Illinois	6,025,415	261,452	4.3	2,358,188	39.1	3,405,775	56.5
Indiana	3,563,524	176,260	4.9	2,070,469	58.1	1,316,795	37.0
Iowa	1,846,332	94,574	5.1	821,104	44.5	930,654	50.4
Kansas	1,681,665	80,984	4.8	712,445	42.4	888,236	52.9
Kentucky	1,656,267	192,268	11.6	1,069,039	64.5	394,960	23.8
Louisiana	2,416,437	277,627	11.5	1,331,213	55.1	807,597	33.4
Maine	779,817	49,681	6.4	391,503	50.2	338,633	43.4
Maryland	3,223,020	164,249	5.1	1,241,094	38.5	1,817,678	56.4
Massachusetts	4,103,291	201,765	4.9	1,850,688	45.1	2,050,838	50.0
Michigan	7,242,874	425,532	5.9	2,525,785	34.9	4,291,557	59.3
Minnesota	3,101,661	131,723	4.2	1,765,775	56.9	1,204,163	38.8
Mississippi	1,076,279	112,610	10.5	701,829	65.2	261,840	24.3

Table 3 - continued

	Total	Amount	%	Amount	%	Amount	%
Missouri	2,749,630	172,986	6.3	1,132,198	41.2	1,444,447	52.5
Montana	632,958	53,807	8.5	302,825	47.8	276,325	43.7
Nebraska	1,005,585	61,695	6.1	226,670	22.5	717,221	71.3
Nevada	595,821	26,432	4.4	235,572	39.5	333,817	56.0
New Hampshire	647,069	21,828	3.4	38,076	5.9	587,165	90.7
New Jersey	6,592,990	290,771	4.4	2,837,625	43.0	3,464,594	52.5
New Mexico	1,008,277	123,188	12.2	757,266	75.1	127,823	12.7
New York	15,757,034	762,061	4.8	6,688,733	42.4	8,306,241	52.7
North Carolina	3,473,998	274,713	7.9	2,294,416	66.0	904,870	26.0
North Dakota	421,752	39,714	9.4	214,063	50.8	167,975	39.8
Ohio	6,293,631	348,846	5.5	3,122,676	49.6	2,822,109	44.8
Oklahoma	1,727,848	95,973	5.6	1,097,712	63.5	534,163	30.9
Oregon	1,863,501	123,033	6.6	522,195	28.0	1,218,273	65.4
Pennsylvania	8,259,284	418,455	5.1	3,825,204	46.3	4,015,625	48.6
Rhode Island	630,222	28,235	4.5	268,310	42.6	333,677	52.9
South Carolina	1,987,657	175,915	8.9	1,113,738	56.0	698,004	35.1
South Dakota	417,550	49,341	11.8	113,409	27.2	254,800	61.0
Tennessee	2,063,971	228,487	11.1	918,665	44.5	916,820	44.4
Texas	11,900,931	846,464	7.1	5,603,133	47.1	5,451,335	45.8
Utah	1,153,256	69,986	6.1	627,118	54.4	456,252	39.6
Vermont	388,013	19,738	5.1	133,284	34.4	234,990	60.6
Virginia	(3)	(3)	(3)	(3)	(3)	(3)	(3)
Washington	3,118,233	196,047	6.3	2,258,430	72.4	663,756	21.3
West Virginia	1,237,866	93,293	7.5	864,138	69.8	280,434	22.7
Wisconsin	3,303,237	154,314	4.7	1,141,259	34.5	2,007,664	60.8
Wyoming	609,195	22,551	3.7	261,877	43.0	324,767	53.3
Outlying areas							
American Samoa	20,479	13,523	66.0	—	—	6,956	34.0
Guam	92,078	10,709	11.6	—	—	81,369	88.4
Northern Marianas	14,908	5,180	34.7	—	—	9,728	65.3
Puerto Rico	936,115	280,937	30.0	—	—	655,178	70.0
Virgin Islands	99,249	17,425	17.6	—	—	81,824	82.4

[1]Includes revenues from local and intermediate sources, gifts, and tuition and fees from patrons.

[2]Includes estimates for the nonreporting state.

[3]Data not reported.

—Data not available or not applicable.

NOTES—Excludes revenues for state education agencies. Because of rounding details may not add to totals.

SOURCE: U.S. Department of Education, National Center for Education Statistics, op. cit.; and Common Core of Data survey. (This table was prepared November 1988.)

Table 4

PER-PUPIL OPERATING EXPENDITURES BY DISTRICT GROUPINGS, NEW YORK STATE: 1972-73 TO 1989-90

| School Year | New York City | District Percentiles* All Major Districts (Excluding New York City) | | | | | Difference 10th & 90th Percentiles | Difference as a Percent of 10th Percentile |
		10	25	50	75	90		
1989-90	$5,093	$3,953	$4,221	$4,740	$6,282	$8,218	$4,265	107.9 %
1988-89	4,763	3,667	3,902	4,374	5,837	7,580	3,913	106.7
1987-88	4,437	3,357	3,587	3,981	5,433	6,962	3,605	107.4
1986-87	4,125	3,025	3,237	3,628	4,673	6,236	3,211	106.1
1985-86	3,802	2,762	2,940	3,287	4,309	5,811	3,049	110.4
1984-85	3,388	2,482	2,680	2,989	3,974	5,211	2,729	110.0
1983-84	3,178	2,298	2,477	2,768	3,597	4,730	2,432	105.8
1982-83	3,010	2,131	2,297	2,566	3,251	4,278	2,147	100.8
1981-82	2,607	1,947	2,079	2,332	2,989	3,865	1,918	98.5
1980-81	2,296	1,796	1,927	2,139	2,756	3,548	1,752	97.6
1979-80	2,432	1,641	1,766	1,956	2,536	3,163	1,522	92.7
1978-79	2,157	1,410	1,512	1,664	2,128	2,757	1,347	95.5
1977-78	2,090	1,319	1,417	1,566	1,971	2,539	1,220	92.5
1976-77	1,979	1,233	1,320	1,471	1,821	2,412	1,179	95.6
1975-76	1,895	1,166	1,242	1,373	1,713	2,148	1,032	88.5
1974-75	1,944	1,067	1,142	1,274	1,593	2,013	946	88.7
1973-74	1,702	975	1,029	1,136	1,431	1,787	812	83.3
1972-73	1,433	931	987	1,086	1,338	1,649	718	77.1

* The value of the district at the percentile shown below is listed.

SOURCE: *Analysis of School Finances in New York State School Districts, 1989-90*, Albany: State Education Department, October 1991. Table 8, p. 12.

Table 5
NEW YORK STATE OPERATING AID FORMULA:
1989-1990

A district's operating aid is determined by first calculating its "formula aid" and comparing it with the minimum "flat grant" guarantee. Growth aid is added for any district eligible as a result of an increase in the district's average daily attendance. The resulting sum is then compared against the minimum apportionment (save-harmless) provisions.

BASIC FORMULA AID (includes flat grant)

Education Law, Section 3602, Subdivision 12
    Each district receives the greater of:
    (i)   Formula Operating Aid; or
    (ii) $360 x Selected TAPU (flat grant provision)
Formula Operating Aid = $3,576 x Operating Aid Ration x Selected TAPU for
    payment
Operating Aid Ratio = 1— (combined wealth ratio x .64)
Combined Wealth Ratio = .5 x district 1985 full value/1985-86 TWPU
                        State Average Full Value/TWPU
                        ($108,400)
                        +
                        .5 x district 1985 adjusted gross income/
                        1985-86
                        State Average Income/TWPU
                        ($55,700)

GROWTH AID

Education Law, Section 3602, Subdivision 13
    For any district whose growth index is greater than 100 percent, the   dis-
    trict also receives growth aid.
Growth Aid = (growth index–100 percent) x basic formula aid
Growth Index = 1987-88 estimated average daily attendance
                1986-87 average daily attendance
Minimum Apportionment
Education Law, Section 3602, Subdivision 18
    A district receives the greater of:
    (i)   The total of formula, flat grant, and growth aid, or
    (ii)   Operating aids base (save-harmless provision)

SOURCE: New York State Education Department, Albany, New York.

Table 6
PROGRAMS FINANCED THROUGH GENERAL SUPPORT FOR PUBLIC SCHOOLS, NEW YORK STATE: 1989-90 AND 1990-91

AID CATEGORY	1989-90 School Year	1990-91 School Year	Change Amount	Change Percent
	(------- Amounts in Millions -------)			
I. Computerized Aids:				
Operating	$4,769.14	$4,894.51	$125.37	2.63
Excellence in Teaching (Districts)	150.57	152.69	2.12	1.41
Early Grade Intervention	13.75	13.93	0.18	1.31
Supplemental Support	400.50	429.40	28.90	7.22
Diagnostic Screening	10.00	10.12	0.12	1.20
Gifted & Talented	13.34	13.32	-0.02	-0.15
Atten. Improvmt./Dropout Prev.	52.42	52.57	0.15	0.29
Limited English Proficiency	26.67	33.80	7.13	26.73
High Tax	191.01	218.04	27.03	14.15
High Tax and SSA Transition	11.07	0.00	-11.07	-100.00
Excess Cost-Private	54.47	55.08	0.61	1.12
Excess Cost-Public	770.55	845.09	74.54	9.67
ERSSA	14.26	14.46	0.20	1.40
Speech Therapy	1.84	1.93	0.09	4.89
BOCES	210.23	232.96	22.73	10.81
Transportation	824.88	871.33	46.45	5.63
Building	272.92	301.87	28.95	10.61
Reorganization Incentive	12.70	12.72	0.02	0.16
Special Services: Occupational Ed	76.98	77.02	0.04	0.05
Computer Admin.	16.33	25.25	8.92	54.62

Table 6 - continued

Computer Hardware	10.04	10.09	0.05	0.50
Textbooks (Incl. Lottery)	75.68	75.03	-0.65	-0.86
Computer Software	9.05	9.09	0.04	0.44
Library Materials	6.03	6.06	0.03	0.50
Voc. Ed. Equipment	5.63	5.63	0.00	0.00
PCEN	81.39	119.84	38.45	47.24
Low Wealth Guarantee	2.36	0.00	-2.36	-100.00
Subtotal	$8,083.81	$8,481.83	$398.02	4.92 %
II. Grant Programs and Other Aid Categories:				
Excess Cost-Private/Rome & Batavia	$0.00	$6.30	$6.30	NA %
Aid to Small City School Dists.	103.25	105.57	2.32	2.25
Excellence in Teaching (BOCES)	7.71	7.90	0.19	2.46
Urban-Suburban Transfer	1.17	1.26	0.09	7.69
Employment Preparation Education	42.15	45.07	2.92	6.93
Homeless Pupils	3.50	4.00	0.50	14.29
Incarcerated Youth	2.20	2.20	0.00	0.00
Reorganization Study Grants	0.47	0.47	0.00	0.00
Building BANs/New Debt Service	39.65	55.00	15.35	38.71
Asbestos	1.75	0.00	-1.75	-100.00
Asbestos: Public/Nonpublic	5.00	0.00	-5.00	-100.00
Asbestos Inspection	25.00	0.00	-25.00	-100.00
Bilingual	9.95	10.95	1.00	10.05
Categorical Reading	38.95	38.95	0.00	0.00
Improving Pupil Performance	22.35	28.35	6.00	26.85
Fort Drum	2.50	2.63	0.13	5.20
Mentor - Interns	12.50	16.50	4.00	32.00

Table 6 - continued

AID CATEGORY	1989-90 School Year	1990-91 School Year	Change	
			Amount	Percent
	(--------- Amounts in Millions ---------)			
Yonkers EIT	1.00	1.00	0.00	0.00
Magnet Schools	56.05	60.05	4.00	7.14
Education of OMH/OMR Pupils	21.00	24.00	3.00	14.29
CIMS	5.50	5.50	0.00	0.00
PCEN Grants	$5.19	$7.14	$1.95	37.57 %
Student Information Systems	9.00	9.00	0.00	0.00
AI/DP Grants	1.60	1.44	-0.16	-10.00
Special School Districts	0.70	0.70	0.00	0.00
Chargebacks	-11.71	-13.38	-1.67	-14.26
Adjusted GSPS TOTAL	$8,490.24	$8,902.43	$412.19	4.85 %
CVEEB	0.65	0.65	0.00	0.00
Special Cat. Projects	12.00	12.00	0.00	0.00
Allowance for Prior Year Adjs.	20.00	20.00	0.00	0.00
SCHOOL YEAR TOTAL	$8,522.89	$8,935.08	$412.19	4.84 %
Additional Prior Year Adjs.	39.92			
Grand Total - New York State	$8,562.81			

Table 7
NEW YORK STATE PER-PUPIL AID AND TOTAL PER-PUPIL EXPENDITURES WITH PERCENT INCREASE: 1972-73 TO 1989-90[a]

School Year	State Aid Per Enrolle Pupil	Percent Increase in State Aid Per Enrolled Pupil	Total General and Special Aid Fund Expenditures Per Enrolled Pupil	Percent Increase in TGFE Per Enrolled Pupil Over Prior Year
1989-90[b]	$3,101[c]	2.5%	$7,502[c]	4.2%
1989-90[b]	3,371[d]	5.9	7,772[d]	8.0
1988-89[e]	3,182	10.8	7,199	9.7
1987-88	2,872	11.6	6,562	9.8
1986-87	2,574	11.7	5,972	7.6
1985-86	2,303	10.5	5,549	10.2
1984-85	2,084	13.7	5,034	7.9
1983-84	1,833	6.8	4,665	9.3
1982-83	1,716	11.1	4,269	8.5
1981-82	1,544	11.5	3,933	12.7
1980-81	1,385	14.0	3,490	11.8
1979-80	1,215	11.3	3,122	10.8
1978-79	1,092	11.5	2,817	8.3
1977-78	979	5.3	2,601	9.6
1976-77	930	3.2	2,374	6.5
1975-76	901	5.6	2,230	3.3
1974-75	739	15.4	2,158	11.6
1973-74	739	5.9	1,933	13.2
1972-73	698	---	1,708	---

[a] For comparisons prior to the 1972-73 school year, the reader is referred to the "Analysis of School Finances, 1979-80."

[b] Estimated.

[c] With TRS maximum deduct of $684 million from totals; does not include possible prepayment by individual school districts.

[d] Anticipated state aid and TGFE prior to deferral of 1989-90 TRS payments.

[e] Preliminary.

SOURCE: New York State Education Department estimates of November 1, 1990, Albany, New York.

Table 8
NEW YORK CITY SHARE OF TOTAL STATE
EDUCATION AID:
1965-66 TO 1988-89

School Year	Total State Aid All Districts	State Aid to New York City	% of State Aid to New York
1965-66	1,266,983,119	308,189,289	24.3
1966-67	1,453,946,281	350,546,625	24.1
1967-68	1,635,054,069	412,582,465	25.2
1968-69	1,986,676,648	549,616,876	27.7
1969-70	2,057,992,955	562,007,652	27.3
1970-71	2,333,368,055	608,739,640	26.1
1971-72	2,378,983,221	601,248,523	25.3
1972-73	2,445,564,828	634,176,614	25.9
1973-74	2,559,873,108	664,246,745	25.9
1974-75	2,930,783,193	794,194,585	27.1
1975-76	3,070,886,901	804,787,724	26.2
1976-77	3,100,559,867	837,936,148	27.0
1977-78	3,142,598,229	859,836,851	27.1
1978-79	3,378,025,297	941,712,024	27.9
1979-80	3,602,442,848	1,012,533,310	28.1
1981-82	4,272,493,477	1,266,420,711	29.6
1982-83	4,644,807,891	1,410,466,437	30.4
1983-84*	4,868,000,000	1,482,000,000	30.4
1984-85*	5,422,000,000	1,783,000,000	32.9
1984-85	5,479,365,133	1,751,646,244	32.0
1985-86	5,998,932,452	1,921,055,540	32.0
1986-87	6,656,238,497	2,162,603,080	32.5
1987-88	7,382,233,516	2,413,887,433	32.7
1988-89	8,094,246,652	2,669,432,563	33.0

* Estimates.

SOURCE: New York State Education Department, Albany, New York.

Table 9
REAL PROPERTY WEALTH CHARACTERISTICS OF DEMOCRATIC ASSEMBLY DISTRICTS OUTSIDE OF NEW YORK CITY: 1985

Total Number of Assembly Districts Outside of New York City Represented by Democrats	Percentage of Assembly District Population Below State Average School Real Property Full Value Per Pupil* ($88,000)
12	90 - 100
7	80 - 89
2	70 - 79
1	60 - 69
4	40 - 49
3	30 - 39
1	20 - 29
1	10 - 19
0	0 - 9
TOTAL 37	

* Weighted Average Daily Attendance.

SOURCE: Legislative Task Force on Demographic Research and Reapportionment, New York State, Albany, New York. (Computations are the authors'.)

Table 10
CONFLICTING EDUCATIONAL FINANCE
DECISIONS OF STATE HIGH COURTS

State	Citation	Consti-tutional	Unconstitutional Under: Equal Protection Clause	Education Clause
Arizona	*Shofstall v. Hollins,* 110 Ariz. 88, 515 P.2d 590 (1973) (en banc)	X		
Arkansas	*Dupree v. Alma School District No. 30,* 279 Ark. 340, 651 S.W.2d 90 (1983)		X	
Califor-nia	*Serrano v. Priest,* 18 Cal. 3d 728, 135 Cal. Rptr. 345, 557 P.2d 929 (1976), *cert. denied,* 432 U.S. 907 (1977) *(Serrano II)*		X	
Colorado	*Lujan v. Colorado State Board of Education,* 649 P.2d 1005 (Colo. 1982)	X		
Connec-ticut	*Horton v. Meskill,* 172 Conn. 615, 376 A.2d 359 (1977) *(Horton I)*		X	X
Georgia	*McDaniel v. Thomas,* 248 Ga. 632, 285 S.E.2d 156 (1981)		X	

Table 10 - continued

State	Citation	Consti-tutional	Unconstitutional Under: Equal Protection Clause	Education Clause
Idaho	*Thompson v. Engelking,* 96 Idaho 793, 537 P.2d 635 (1975)	X		
Illinois	*Blase v. State,* 55 Ill. 2d 94, 302 N.E.2d 46 (1973)	X		
Kentucky	*Rose v. Council for Better Education, Inc.,* 790 S.W.2d 186 (Ky. 1989)			X
Maryland	*Hornbeck v. Somerset County Board of Education,* 295 Md. 597, 458 A.2d 758 (1983)	X		
Michigan	*Milliken v. Green,* 390 Mich. 389, 212 N.W.2d 711 (1973)	X		
Montana	*Helena Elementary School District. No. 1 v. State,* 769 P.2d 684 (Mont. 1989)			X
New Jersey	*Robinson v. Cahill,* 62 N.J. 473, 303 A.2d 273, *cert. denied,* 414 U.S. 976 (1973) *(Robinson I)*			X

Table 10 - continued

State	Citation	Consti-tutional	Unconstitutional Under: Equal Protection Clause	Education Clause
New York	*Board of Education, Levittown Union Free School District v. Nyquist* 57 N.Y.2d 27, 453 N.Y.S. 2d 643, 439 N.E. 2d 359 (1982), *appeal dismissed,* 459 U.S. 1139 (1983)	X		
North Carolina	*Britt v. North Carolina State Board of Education,* 86 N.C. App. 282, 357 S.E. 2d 432, *appeal dismissed mem.,* 320 N.C. 790, 361 S.E.2d 71 (1987)	X		
Ohio	*Board of Education of the City School District of the City of Cincinnati v. Walter,* 58 Ohio St. 2d 368, 390 N.E.2d 813 (1979), *cert. denied,* 444 U.S. 1015 (1980)	X		
Okla-homa	*Fair School Finance Council, Inc. v. State,* 746 P.2d 1135 (Okla. 1987)	X		
Oregon	*Olsen v. State,* 276 Or. 9, 554 P.2d 139 (1976)	X		

Table 10 - continued

State	Citation	Consti-tutional	Unconstitutional Under: Equal Protection Clause	Education Clause
Pennsyl-vania	*Danson v. Casey,* 484 Pa. 415, 399 A.2d 360 (1979)	X		
South Carolina	*Richland County v. Campbell,* 294 S.C. 346, 364 S.E.3d 470 (1988)	X		
Texas	*Edgewood Independent School District v. Kirby,* 777 S.W.2d 391 (Tex. 1989)			X
Washing-ton	*Seattle School District No. 1 v. State,* 90 Wash. 2d 476, 585 P.2d 71 (1978)			X
West Virginia	*Pauley v. Kelly,* 162 W. Va. 672, 255 S.E.2d 859 (1979)		X	X
Wiscon-sin	*Kukor v. Grover,* 148 Wis. 2d 469, 436 N.W.2d 568 (1989)	X		
Wyoming	*Washakie County School District No. 1 v. Herschler,* 606 P.2d 310 (Wyo.), *cert. denied,* 449 U.S. 824 (1980)		X	

Chart 1
CONTRASTING APPROACHES TO EDUCATIONAL
OPPORTUNITY

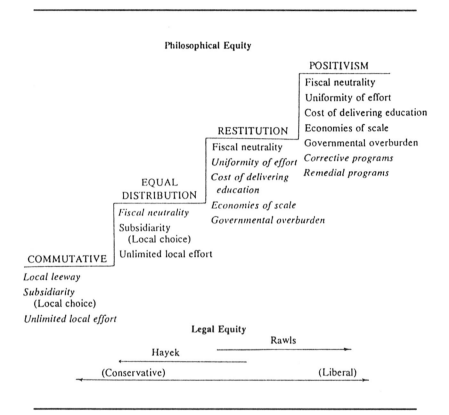

SOURCE: Kern Alexander, "Concepts of Equity," in Walter W. McMahon and Terry G. Geske, eds., *Financing Education: Overcoming Inefficiency and Inequity*, Urbana: University of Illinois Press, 1982, p. 211. Reprinted by permission of publishers.

Chart 2
EXPENDITURE INEQUALITIES IN NEW YORK STATE:
1974-75 TO 1986-87

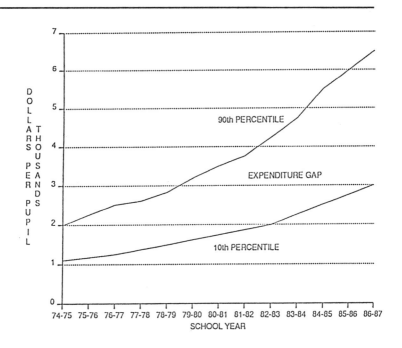

	74-75	75-76	76-77	77-78	78-79	79-80	80-81	81-82	82-83	83-84	84-85	85-86	86-87
90th PCTL	$2045	2227	2436	2631	2838	3156	3548	3865	4278	4732	5211	5789	6198
10th PCTL	$1088	1189	1253	1347	1448	1566	1797	1947	2131	2298	2482	2756	2948
Exp. Gap	88%	87%	94%	95%	96%	102%	97%	99%	100%	105%	110%	110%	110%

SOURCE: New York State Education Department, Albany, New York.

BIBLIOGRAPHY

Alexander, Kern. "Concepts of Equity." In Walter W. McMahon and Terry G. Geske (eds.), *Financing Education: Overcoming Inefficiency and Inequity.* Urbana: University of Illinois Press, 1982.

Alexander, Kern, and K. Forbis Jordan. *Constitutional Reform of School Finance.* Lexington, Mass.: Lexington Books, 1973.

Alsop, Joseph. *FDR: A Centenary Remembrance.* New York: Viking Press, 1982.

Anderson, William R. "School Finance Litigation: The Styles of Judicial Intervention." *Washington Law Review* 55 (1979), p. 137.

_____. "State School Finance Litigation." *The Urban Lawyer* 14 (1982), p. 383.

Bawden, D. Lee, and John L. Palmer. "Society Policy: Changing the Welfare State." In John L. Palmer and Isabel V. Sawhill (eds.), *The Reagan Record.* Cambridge, Mass.: Ballinger Pub. Co., 1984.

Berke, Joel S. *Answers to Inequity: An Analysis of the New School Finance.* Berkeley, Calif.: McCutchan Pub. Corp., 1974.

Berke, Joel S., and John J. Callahan. "*Serrano v. Priest:* Milestone or Millstone for School Finance." *Journal of Public Law* 21 (1972), p. 23.

Berke, Joel S., and Richard J. Coley. *Politicians, Judges, and City Schools: Reforming School Finance in New York.* New York: Russell Sage Foundation, 1984.

Berne, Robert, and Leanna Stiefel. *The Measurement of Equity in School Finance: Conceptual, Methodological and Empirical Dimensions.* Baltimore: The Johns Hopkins University Press, 1984.

Bisch, Robert L. "Fiscal Equalization through Court Decisions: Policy Making without Evidence." In Eleanor Ostrom (ed.), *The Delivery of Urban Services.* Berkeley, Calif.: Sage Publications, 1976.

Buriup, Percy E. *Financing Education in a Climate of Change.* 3d ed. Boston: Allyn and Bacon, 1982.

Burke, Arvid. "Development of Public School Finance in New York State." Occasional Paper 14. New York State Finance Law Study, Albany, N.Y., Vol. 5, 1978.

Chambers, Julius. "Adequate Education for All: A Right, An Achievable Goal. *Harvard Civil Rights - Civil Liberties Law Review* 22 (1987), p. 55.

Coleman, James S., *The Concept of Equal Educational Opportunity.* Cambridge, Mass.: Harvard University Press, 1969.

Coleman, James S., et. al. *Equality of Educational Opportunity.* Washington, D.C.: Government Printing Office, 1966.

Coons, John E. "'Fiscal Neutrality' after *Rodriguez.*" *Law and Contemporary Problems* 38 (1974), p. 299.

————. "Recent Trends in Science Fiction: *Serrano* among the People of Number." *Journal of Law and Education* 6 (1977), p. 23.

Coons, John E., William H. Clune and Stephen D. Sugarman. *Private Wealth and Public Education.* Cambridge, Mass.: Harvard University Press, 1970.

Crockett, Ulysses S., Jr. "Financing Public Education in New York State: The *Levittown* Decision and Its Challenge to the State Legislature." *The Urban Lawyer* 15 (1983), p. 29.

Cubberly, Ellwood P. *School Funds and Their Apportionment.* New York: Columbia University Teachers College, 1905.

Elmore, Richard F., and Milbery Wallin McLaughlin. *Reform and Retrenchment: The Politics of California School Finance Reform.* Cambridge, Mass.: Ballinger Pub. Co., 1982.

Friedman, Herbert, and Michael Wiseman. "Understanding the Equity Consequences of School-Finance Reform." *Harvard Educational Review* 48, No. 2 (May 1978), pp. 193-226.

Garms, Walter I., James W. Guthrie and Lawrence C. Pierce. *School Finance: The Economics and Politics of Public Education.* Englewood Cliffs, N.J.: Prentice-Hall, 1978.

Grubb, Norton W., and Jack W. Osman. "The Causes of School Finance Inequalities: *Serrano* and the Case of California." *Public Finance Quarterly* 5 (1977), p. 373.

Harrison, Russell S. *Equality in Public School Finance.* Lexington, Mass.: Lexington Books, 1976.

Harvith, Bernard E. "Education Law." *Syracuse Law Review* 34 (1983), p. 215.

Hayek, Friedrich A. *Law, Legislation and Liberty.* 3 Vols. Chicago: University of Chicago Press, 1973-79.

Holmes, Oliver Wendell. In Mark DeWolfe (ed.), *The Common Law.* Cambridge, Mass.: Harvard University Press, 1963.

Hughes, Charles Evans. *Addresses and Papers of Charles Evan Hughes.* New York: Putnam, 1908.

Jencks, Christopher, et al. *Inequality: A Reassessment of the Effect of Family and Schooling in America.* New York: Basic Books, 1972.

Kirp, David L., and Mark G. Yudof. *Educational Policy and the Law: Cases and Materials.* 2d ed. Berkeley, Calif.: McCutchan Pub. Corp., 1982. Plus

1984 supplement.

Kohlberg, Lawrence. *The Philosophy of Moral Development: Moral Stages and the Idea of Justice.* New York: Harper & Row, 1981.

Lehne, Richard. *The Quest for Justice: The Politics of School Finance.* New York: Longman, 1978.

LeRoy, Erik. "The Egalitarian Roots of the Education Article of the Wisconsin Constitution: Old History, New Interpretation, *Buse v. Smith* Criticized." *Wisconsin Law Review* 6 (1981), p. 1325.

Lineberry, Robert L. *Equality and Urban Policy.* Beverly Hills, Calif.: Sage Publications, 1977.

Malone, Paul. *The Fiscal Aspects of State and Local Relationships in New York.* Albany: New York State Tax Commission, 1937.

McMahon, Walter W., and Terry G. Geske (eds.). *Financing Education: Overcoming Inefficiency and Inequity.* Urbana: University of Illinois Press, 1982.

Ment, David M. *Equality Concerns Reflected in the Establishment and Development of New York State's Public Education System,* submitted as Appendix D to City-Plaintiffs' Court of Appeals brief in *Levittown v. Nyquist,* April 16, 1982.

Michelman, Frank I. "Forward: The Supreme Court 1968 Term." *Harvard Law Review* 83 (1969), p. 7.

_____. "In Pursuit of Constitutional Welfare Rights: One View of Rawls' Theory of Justice." *University of Pennsylvania Law Review* 121 (1973), p. 962.

Morrison, Henry C. *School Revenue.* Chicago: University of Chicago Press, 1930.

Mort, Paul R., and Walter C. Reusser. *Public School Finance.* New York: McGraw-Hill, 1941.

Moynihan, Daniel P., and Frederick Mosteller, (eds.). *On Equality of Educational Opportunity.* New York: Random House, 1972.

Mueller, Van D., and Mary P. McKeown (eds.). *The Fiscal, Legal, and Political Aspects of State Reform of Elementary and Secondary Education.* Cambridge, Mass.: Ballinger Pub. Co., 1986.

Murray, Charles. *Losing Ground: American Social Policy, 1950-1980.* New York: Basic Books, 1984.

New York State Commission on the Quality, Cost and Financing of Elementary and Secondary Education. 3 Vols. Albany: The Commission, 1972.

New York State Special Task Force on Equity and Excellence in Education, Report and Recommendations of the. Albany, N.Y., February 1982.

"Note. To Render Them Safe: The Analysis of State Constitutional Provisions in Public School Finance Reform Litigation." *Virginia Law Review* 75 (1989), p. 1639.

Nwabuogu, Michael N. "On the Meaning and Application of Equal Educational Opportunity: A Review Article." *Journal of Education Finance* 10, No. 1 (Summer 1984).

Pincus, John. *The Serrano Case: Policy for Education or for Public Finance.*

Santa Monica, Calif.: The Rand Corp., 1977.

President's Commission on School Finance. *Schools, People, and Money: The Need for Educational Reform.* Washington, D.C.: Government Printing Office, 1972.

Preovolos, Penelope A. "*Rodriguez* Revisited: Federalism, Meaningful Access, and the Right to Adequate Education." *Santa Clara Law Review* 20 (1980), p. 75.

Ratner, Gershon M. "A New Legal Duty for Urban Public Schools: Effective Education in Basic Skills." *Texas Law Review* 63 (1985), p. 5.

Rawls, John. *A Theory of Justice.* Cambridge, Mass.: Harvard University Press, 1971.

Sacks, Seymour. *City Schools/Suburban Schools: A History of Fiscal Impact.* Syracuse: Syracuse University Press, 1972.

Scheuer, Joan. "The Equity of New York State's System of Financing Schools: An Update." *Journal of Education Finance* 9, No. 1 (Summer 1983).

_____. *State Aid for Schools: A Handbook for Policy Makers.* New York: New York City Board of Education, January 1985.

Scott, Nelson, "Wealth Classification and Equal Protection: Quo Vadimus?" *Houston Law Review* 19 (1982), p. 713.

Shalala, Donna G. "School Finance in New York State." In Joel S. Berke, Alan K. Campbell and Robert J. Goettel (eds.), *Financing Equal Educational Opportunity: Alternatives for School Finance.* Berkeley, Calif.: Mc-Cutchan Pub. Corp., 1974.

Shanks. Hershel. "Educational Financing and Equal Protection: Will the California Supreme Court's Breakthrough Become the Law of the Land?" *Journal of Law and Education* (1972), p. 73.

Shulman, L., and A. Syliss (eds.). *Handbook of Teaching and Policy.* New York: Longman, 1983.

Strayer, George D., and Robert M. Haig. *The Financing of Education in the State of New York.* New York: Macmillan, 1923.

Sugarman, Stephen D. "A Judicial Prod to Legislative Reform of Educational Finance." *Planning and Change* 2 (1972), p. 180.

Tho, William E. "The Third Wave: The Impact of the Montana, Kentucky, and Texas Decisions on the Future of Public School Finance Reform Litigation." *Journal of Law and Education* 19 (1990), p. 219.

Wilson, Lois, and Joan Gavrilik. "Education Aid in New York State: Targeting Issues and Measures." *Publius: The Journal of Federalism* 19 (1989), p. 95.

Wise, Arthur E. "Educational Adequacy: A Concept in Search of Meaning." *Journal of Education Finance* 8, No. 3 (Winter 1981), p. 301.

_____. *Rich Schools, Poor Schools: The Promise of Equal Educational Opportunity.* Chicago: University of Chicago Press, 1967.

INDEX

ganization of, as a barrier to equalization, 34; legislative interest in, 59-60, 68. *See also* Counties; Educational opportunity; Public schools; State Aid

Schools. *See* Public Schools

Serrano, John, 74

Serrano I-II, 74-76, 84

"Setting Priorities for New York State," 99

Smith, Al, 99

Smith, L. Kingsley (Justice), 78-80, 98

State: full funding of education by, 35-36, 111, 128, 133

State aid: to achieve fiscal equality, 11; and fiscal disparities, 50-51, 61, 66, 100-102; and public education, 9, 14-15, 17, 20, 23, 26, 28-34, 47-48, 121. *See also* Aid formulas; Legislature; Political process

State courts: legal challenges to educational funding, 77-81. *See also* specific states

State Superintendent of Instruction, 24

Stavisky, Leonard, 95-96

Strict scrutiny standard, 73-76, 90

Syracuse (New York), 39

Texas Supreme Court, 90, 112

United States Constitution: Fourteenth Amendment, 72

United States Supreme Court, 17, 73, 75-76, 81, 88, 92, 106, 132

Wachtler, Sol, 82

Wealth. *See* Money and Wealth.

West Virginia: legal challenges to educational funding, 87-88, 91, 108

West Virginia Supreme Court, 87

Wilson, Lois, 64

Wilson, Malcolm (Governor), 49, 77

Wise, Arthur, 71

Yonkers (New York), 39